Planning Law and Practice

Available titles in this series include:

Agricultural Tenancies
Angela Sydenham

Change of Name
Nasreen Pearce

Charities and Not-for-Profit Entities
Cecile Gillard

Child Care and Protection
Barbara Mitchels (editor) with Julie Doughty, Helen James and Safda Mahmood

Debt Recovery in the Courts
John Kruse

Partnership and LLP Law
Elspeth Berry

Personal Injury Litigation
Gordon Exall

Procedure in Civil Courts and Tribunals
John Bowers QC and Eleena Misra

Residential Tenancies
Richard Colbey and Niamh O'Brien

Termination of Employment
John Bowers QC and Carol Davis

 Wildy Practice Guides

Planning Law and Practice

David Travers QC,
Noémi Byrd and
Giles Atkinson

Wildy, Simmonds and Hill Publishing

© David Travers QC, Noémi Byrd and Giles Atkinson, 2013

Contains public sector information licensed under the Open Government Licence v1.0

ISBN 9780854901159

British Library Cataloguing in Publication Data

A catalogue record for this book is available from the British Library

The right of David Travers QC, Noémi Byrd and Giles Atkinson to be identified as the authors of this Work has been asserted by them in accordance with the Copyright, Designs and Patents Act 1988.

All rights reserved. No part of this book may be reproduced, stored in a retrieval system, or transmitted, in any form or by any means, electronic, mechanical, photocopying, recording or otherwise, without the consent of the copyright owners, application for which should be addressed to the publisher. Such a written permission must also be obtained before any part of this publication is stored in a retrieval system of any nature.

This Work is published for general guidance only and is not intended as a substitute for professional advice. While every care has been taken in the preparation of the text, the publishers and authors can accept no responsibility for the consequences of any errors, however caused.

First published in 2013 by

Wildy, Simmonds & Hill Publishing
58 Carey Street
London WC2A 2JF
England
www.wildy.com

Typeset by Cornubia Press Ltd, Bristol.
Printed in Great Britain by CPI Group (UK) Ltd, Croydon, CR0 4YY.

In Memoriam
Peter Harrison QC
1965–2013

Contents

Foreword   xiii

1	**Overview of the Planning System of England and Wales**	**1**
	1.1 Brief history of the major planning Acts	1
	1.2 Town and Country Planning Act 1947	1
	1.3 Town and Country Planning Act 1990	3
	1.4 Planning and Compulsory Purchase Act 2004	4
	1.5 Planning Act 2008	6
	1.6 Localism Act 2011	6
	1.7 How the planning system is organised	7
	1.7.1 Secretary of State	8
	Plan-making	8
	1.7.2 Powers since 2004	9
	1.7.3 Secretary of State's intervention	10
	1.8 Appeals	11
	1.8.1 Called in applications	12
	1.8.2 Policy guidance	13
	1.9 Local planning authorities	15
	1.9.1 What is the local planning authority?	15
	1.9.2 What are the functions of the local planning authority?	16
	1.9.3 Plan-making	16
	1.9.4 Development management	18
2	**The Requirement for Planning Permission**	**19**
	2.1 Key concepts	19
	2.2 What is operational development?	20
	2.2.1 Building operations requiring planning permission	20
	What is a 'building'?	20
	Building operations	21
	2.2.2 Demolition	22
	Partial demolition	23
	2.2.3 Permitted demolition of dwelling houses (Class A)	23
	2.3 Permission not required for internal works	24
	2.3.1 What is a 'material impact on the exterior' of a building?	25
	2.3.2 Basements	25

		2.3.3	Driveways	25
		2.3.4	Exceptions to the internal works rule	25
		2.3.5	Engineering operations	26
			Exceptions	26
		2.3.6	Mining operations	26
			Exception for exploratory works	27
	2.4	What is a material change of use?		27
		2.4.1	The planning unit	27
		2.4.2	Types of use	28
		2.4.3	Ancillary uses	28
		2.4.4	Composite uses	29
		2.4.5	Physical separation	30
		2.4.6	Functional separation	30
		2.4.7	What rights flow from the current use?	31
	2.5	When is change material?		31
		2.5.1	Intensification of use as a material change	31
		2.5.2	Intensification of use within the Use Classes Order 1987	32
		2.5.3	Intensification of use not within the Use Classes Order 1987	32
		2.5.4	Intensification of ancillary uses	33
		2.5.5	Flat conversions	33
		2.5.6	Changes within use classes	34
		2.5.7	Sub-classes of use classes	34
			Sui generis use	35
	2.6	Exceptions to the need for planning permission for material change of use		35
		2.6.1	Incidental uses with the curtilage of a dwelling house	35
			What is the curtilage?	36
		2.6.2	Use incidental to the enjoyment of the dwelling house	36
		2.6.3	Use of agricultural land	36
		2.6.4	Ancillary use of agricultural land	37
	2.7	Permitted development rights		37
		2.7.1	Town and Country Planning (General Permitted Development) Order 1995	37
		2.7.2	Directions under article 4 of the Town and Country Planning (General Permitted Development) Order 1995	38
		2.7.3	Schedule 1 to the Town and Country Planning (General Permitted Development) Order 1995	38

				Preface	ix
		2.7.4	Schedule 2 to the Town and Country Planning (General Permitted Development) Order 1995		39
	2.8	Simplified planning zones and enterprise zone schemes			40
	2.9	Certificates of lawfulness			40
		2.9.1	Certificates of lawfulness for proposed use or development		40
		2.9.2	No 'development'		41
		2.9.3	Certificates of lawfulness for existing use or development		42
		2.9.4	Immunity from enforcement action		43
		2.8.5	Failure to comply with a planning condition		44
		2.8.6	Revocation		44
		2.8.7	Appeal against refusal		44
3	**Applying for Planning Permission**				**45**
	3.1	Pre-application consultation with the local planning authority			45
	3.2	Statutory pre-application consultation			47
	3.3	Outline permission			47
	3.4	Expiry of outline permissions			48
	3.5	Application for full permission			49
	3.6	Information requirements			50
	3.7	Site plan			50
	3.8	Particulars			50
	3.9	Design and access statements			51
		3.9.1	Local area requirements		53
		3.9.2	Fees		53
		3.9.3	Validation		54
		3.9.4	Publicity		55
		3.9.5	Register of planning applications		57
	3.10	Consultation			58
		3.10.1	Statutory consultees		58
		3.10.2	Time limits		59
	3.11	Written notice of decision			60
		3.11.1	Retrospective consent		61
	3.12	Conservation area consent			62
	3.13	Listed building consent			63
4	**How Planning Applications are Determined**				**65**
	4.1	Process – who makes the decision?			65
	4.2	Officer report			66

4.3		Conduct of meetings	67
4.4		Delegated authority	67
4.5		Member overturns	69
4.6		Costs against local planning authorities	70
4.7		Powers	70
	4.7.1	The development plan	72
	4.7.2	Material considerations	74
4.8		Government policy – national planning policy framework	75
	4.8.1	Sustainable development	77
	4.8.2	Implementation	78
4.9		Planning obligations and community infrastructure levy	79
	4.9.1	How the Community Infrastructure Levy works	81

5 The Grant of Planning Permission 83

5.1		Legal effect of a planning permission	83
5.2		Interpretation	83
5.3		Effect of a planning permission	84
	5.3.1	Who benefits?	84
	5.3.2	Extent of the permission	84
	5.3.3	Outline planning permission	85
5.4		Duration of a planning permission	85
	5.4.1	When does development begin?	86
	5.4.2	Completion notices	87
5.5		Changes to an existing planning permission	87
	5.5.1	Non-material changes	87
	5.5.2	Revocation of a planning permission	87
5.6		Planning conditions	88
	5.6.1	Planning purpose of conditions	89
	5.6.2	Relationship to the development	89
		Conditions modifying the development	90
	5.6.3	'Grampian' conditions	90
	5.6.4	Personal conditions	91
	5.6.5	Reasonableness	91
		Financial contributions	91
		Private property rights	91
		Uncertainty	92
		Enforceability	93
	5.6.6	Effect of invalid condition	93
	5.6.7	Challenge to planning conditions	94
	5.6.8	Conditions following appeal	94
5.7		Planning permission and other legal interests	94

		5.7.1	Private nuisance	95
		5.7.2	Interference with other easements	96
	5.8	Highways		96
		5.8.1	Orders made by the Secretary of State	96
		5.8.2	Orders made by the local planning authority	96
	5.9	Listed building consent		97
		5.9.1	Extent of a listed building	98
		5.9.2	Definition of the curtilage	98
		5.9.3	Requirement for listed building consent	99
			Effect on character	100
		5.9.4	Exempted listed buildings	101
			Churches	101
			Scheduled ancient monuments	101
		5.9.5	Obtaining consent	101
			Government guidance	102
	5.10	Conservation areas		103
		5.10.1	When is conservation area consent required?	104
			Directions under Article 4 of the Town and Country Planning (General Permitted Development) Order 1995	105
			Local Heritage Lists	105
6	**Appeals against Refusal of Planning Permission**			**107**
	6.1	Refusal of planning permission		107
	6.2	Who can appeal?		107
	6.3	The role of 'third parties'		107
	6.4	Who determines planning appeals?		108
		6.4.1	Recovered jurisdiction	109
	6.5	Deciding to appeal against refusal of planning permission		109
		6.5.1	Does the proposal accord with the development plan?	110
		6.5.2	When and how to appeal	110
			When should the local planning authority issue its decision?	110
			Time limits for appeals	111
			Householder Appeals Service	111
		6.5.3	What to include in an appeal form	112
		6.5.4	Choice of procedure	113
			Written representations	113

		Hearing	113
		Inquiry	113
	6.5.5	Alterations to the proposed scheme	114
6.6	Inquiries procedure		114
	6.6.1	Preliminary stage	114
	6.6.2	Statement of case	115
	6.6.3	Statement of common ground	115
	6.6.4	Proof of evidence	115
	6.6.5	The inquiry	116
6.7	Costs		119
6.8	Inspector's conduct		120
	6.8.1	Inspector's powers on appeal	120
		Giving reasons	120
	6.8.2	Listed building and conservation area appeals	121
	6.8.3	Lawful development certificate appeals	121
6.9	Appeals to the High Court under section 288 of the Town and Country Planning Act 1990		121
	6.9.1	Protective Costs Orders	122
	6.9.2	Interim orders	124

Glossary 125

Foreword

Planning law today is not simple. It extends across a large number of Acts of Parliament and statutory instruments, whose provisions have, in their turn, generated a huge volume of case law. The jurisprudence is dynamic, complex and vast. Continual reform of the system by most of the governments that have held power in the last 65 years has not stifled but has stimulated the ingenuity of planning lawyers, and that is no surprise. The Localism Act 2011 is the latest chapter in a continuing history of change. David Travers QC and his co-authors have produced a concise and informative textbook, in which the practitioner will find a clear and accurate summary of planning law and practice in 2013. The book embraces the principal elements of the planning system, presents them in a convenient and logical format, and provides a crisp commentary on each. I commend it to all who work in this field, and wish it the success it deserves.

The Hon Mr Justice Lindblom
Royal Courts of Justice
March 2013

1 Overview of the Planning System of England and Wales

1.1 Brief history of the major planning Acts

For the purposes of this book the Town and Country Planning Act 1947 (TCPA 1947) represents the advent of the planning system in England and Wales. Before 1947 there had been a number of enactments which sought to regulate in the public interest the way in which landowners could use their own land, but it was the TCPA 1947 which established the framework of the planning system that is still recognisable today.

It is worth noting that the TCPA 1947 was passed by the pioneering Attlee Government, which sought to chart a way out of the post-Second World War devastation and near bankruptcy which enveloped the country. Out of this period came, for example, the momentous National Health Service Act 1946, the Coal Industry Nationalisation Act 1946 and the Electricity Act 1947, which nationalised the electricity supply.

It was within this context of state control and nationalisation that the TCPA 1947 was passed, and at its heart lies the spirit of its time. In essence, what the TCPA 1947 did was to nationalise the right of private landowners to develop their own land. Control by the state of development on private land is quite a radical concept and one that remains today. Unlike almost all of the other industries and services that were nationalised in the post-Second World War period, the regulation of land use remains in the public domain. Perhaps it is for this reason that it continues to be so contentious.

1.2 Town and Country Planning Act 1947

Under pre-Second World War legislation, planning control only took effect if a local authority chose to exercise powers that were available to it. The TCPA 1947 for the first time imposed the system of planning control to take effect automatically across the whole of England and Wales. This was achieved by the establishment of local planning authorities (LPAs), corresponding to existing local authorities. Each LPA was required to survey its area and produce a plan for how land should be used, known as a development plan.

With this obligation to prepare development plans, the responsibility for the 'vision' of how an area should be developed was passed to LPAs. Of course it was necessary at the same time for the TCPA 1947 to both define development and to impose a requirement for anyone wishing to undertake development to seek permission for it. The development plan was then to guide the LPAs' decisions about whether to grant consent for proposed development or to refuse it. In this way the LPA, by reference to its development plan, could seek to achieve the vision for its area as well as to allow a measure of predictability for would-be applicants so that he or she would have some indication in advance whether a proposed scheme would be acceptable to the LPA. These broad concepts remain a central part of the legislation today.

The definition of development as set out at section 12 of the TCPA 1947 was as follows:

> In this Act except where the context otherwise requires, the expression 'development' means the carrying out of building, engineering, mining or other operations in, on, over or under land, or the making of any material change in the use of any buildings or other land.

This definition of development has remained unchanged through the many subsequent amendments to and consolidations of the planning Acts since 1947, and the concept of development, coupled with the requirement of consent for it, remains central to planning control. This is explored further in Chapter 2.

There are many other central elements of the system of planning control introduced by the TCPA 1947 which remain today. Applications for permission are still made to the LPA in whose area the land the subject of the application lies, and if permission is refused or granted subject to conditions with which the applicant is aggrieved, appeal still lies to the responsible government minister, usually now represented by an Inspector.

For any system of planning control to be truly effective it must have provisions for enforcement and the basis of the planning enforcement regime in force today was established in 1947 with LPAs empowered to serve enforcement notices alleging a breach of planning control, against which the recipient has a statutory right of appeal (to the Secretary of State now, rather than to a magistrates' court as in 1947). Failure to comply with an enforcement notice was first made an offence by the TCPA 1947.

The TCPA 1947 was a landmark piece of legislation both in the breadth of its conception, nationalising development rights and in its durability, with much of it still recognisable today. Leaving aside those parts of the TCPA 1947 concerned with compensation or betterment, which are outside the scope of this book, the first clause of the long title to the TCPA 1947 summarises what it was intended to do:

> An Act to make fresh provision for planning the development and use of land, for the grant of permission to develop land and for other powers of control over the use of land

Essentially, this is still what the planning system seeks to do, and what this book seeks to explain.

1.3 Town and Country Planning Act 1990

The Town and Country Planning Act 1990 (TCPA 1990) is the current principal statute dealing with town and country planning. It is the successor to the TCPA 1947 and contains much that was established in the earlier Act. There have been a number of consolidating and amending Acts between 1947 and 1990, indeed the TCPA 1990 is itself a consolidating Act which has subsequently been amended. The bulk of the rest of this book refers to the TCPA 1990.

The TCPA 1990 comprises 337 sections arranged into 15 Parts, with 17 Schedules. This book is concerned with those matters that are most likely to be of interest to the legal practitioner who needs to know how the system works at the 'front end'; that is, when planning permission is likely to be needed, how to apply for it, how an application will be determined, what grant of planning permission allows and, if not granted, how to appeal.

These matters are those dealt with in the first three parts of the TCPA 1990 – Part I Planning Authorities, Part II Development Plans and Part III Control over Development – and it is consequently those parts of the TCPA 1990 that form the subject of this book. Planning enforcement is outside the scope of this book and is dealt with in more detail in the Wildy Practice Guide by David Travers, Edward Grant and Emmaline Lambert, *Planning Enforcement* (Wildy, Simmons & Hill, 2013).

It is important to complete this brief history of the planning system with reference to the following pieces of legislation.

1.4 Planning and Compulsory Purchase Act 2004

For the purposes of this book the principal changes introduced by the Planning and Compulsory Purchase Act 2004 (PCPA 2004) were to the development plan. What currently constitutes the development plan is addressed in more detail in Chapter 4, but it is important to explain the legislative history because in many parts of the country the development plan prepared under earlier legislation remains in force.

From 1968 to the coming into force of the PCPA in 2004 the development plan, which is essentially the LPA's policy against which planning applications are assessed, comprised a two-tier system of structure plans and local plans. A structure plan, usually prepared by a county council, provided a strategic statement of policy, below which sat local plans which provided more detail at the local level and were prepared by district or borough councils. Together, structure plans and local plans constituted the development plan.

In each borough in London and in the great urban conurbations of Greater Manchester, Merseyside, South Yorkshire, Tyne and Wear, West Midlands and West Yorkshire, known as metropolitan authorities, the development plan took a different form, as a Unitary Development Plan (UDP). The UDP essentially combined in one document the strategic element of the structure plan in its Part 1 with the detailed local policies corresponding to the local plan in its Part 2.

Later, UDPs were also produced by other local authorities outside London and the metropolitan areas which became unitary authorities as a result of one of the many local government reorganisations since the Second World War.

The PCPA 2004 dramatically swept away the structure plan and local plan, and UDP forms of the development plan. In their place was introduced a different two-tier system with Regional Strategies providing the strategic level policy and Development Plan Documents the more local policy; since the PCPA 2004 came into force these documents have, subject to their preparation and adoption by the relevant LPAs, comprised the development plan.

With the PCPA 2004 came a sometimes baffling slew of new planning terminology and jargon used to name each part of the new system. Although it is not a phrase that is actually found in the Act itself, the Local Development Framework (LDF) is in practice the term usually used to describe all of the planning documents that an LPA is now required to produce to deliver the spatial planning strategy for its area and the initials LDF are commonly referred to.

Within the LDF sit the Local Development Documents. These, together with the Regional Strategies outside London (until their abolition, see Chapter 4), and any neighbourhood development plans, make up the development plan. Confusingly, what had been known as Local Development Documents were renamed 'Local Plans' by the Town and Country Planning (Local Planning) (England) Regulations 2012 (SI 2012/767) with effect from April 2012.

This renaming of Local Development Documents as Local Plans illustrates well an unfortunate feature of all reform of the planning system by all governments over the years. There is something in the planning system that makes it attractive to politicians who believe it can be reformed to be more efficient, i.e. to deliver speedier decisions with greater certainty and predictability for applicants, or to be more responsive to the wishes of communities, allowing them greater involvement and participation. In fact, reform often seeks to achieve both of these directly contradictory aspirations. The result of this almost constant reform is that the planning system is periodically dismantled and then re-assembled but with each constituent part given a different name, although it performs largely the same role as its predecessor.

The LDF also contains other elements such as supplementary planning documents which do not form part of the development plan but may expand policy or provide more detail. Supplementary planning documents are produced on a range of matters including, for example, the scale and design of residential extensions and alterations that the LPA finds acceptable. Guidance contained in a supplementary planning document is a material consideration to be taken into account in planning appeals.

Within the LDF are a number of other documents that the LPA is required to produce, including a Statement of Community Involvement and a Local Development Scheme; the latter is essentially a plan and timetable for the preparation of the documents themselves that make up the LDF.

What comprises the development plan is addressed in more detail in Chapter 4, but it is important to be aware of how the system has changed from structure plan/local plan and UDP to LDF because the speed with which LPAs – both historically and presently – have managed to prepare and adopt their development plan varies considerably, with the result that in some parts of the country the development plan remains the structure plan/local plan or UDP and in others it may be a Development Plan Document. Given the time that is required to prepare and adopt an LDF, it is often the case that during its preparation the structure plan/local plan or UDP remain the adopted policy but as progress is made in preparing the LDF parts of the framework are adopted, with the result that there are elements of both the old and the new system in force at the same time.

The principal Development Plan Document, and often the first one adopted by an LPA, is the Core Strategy.

1.5 Planning Act 2008

The central change to the planning system introduced by the Planning Act 2008 was the introduction of a new system to deal with nationally significant infrastructure projects (NSIPs), which lies outside the scope of this book. Simply put, the Act created an Infrastructure Planning Commission responsible for examining, and in some cases deciding, whether to grant planning permission for, NSIPs including energy, transport, water and waste infrastructure projects. The Commission was abolished by the Localism Act 2011 and its functions transferred to the Infrastructure Planning Unit within the Planning Inspectorate (PINS).

1.6 Localism Act 2011

Apart from abolishing the relatively newly created Infrastructure Planning Commission, the Localism Act 2011 has imposed a number of significant changes on the planning system in England and Wales. Changes to the plan-making system include the Secretary of State's power under section 109 to abolish Regional Spatial Strategies, in whole or in part. Section 110 imposes on LPAs, county councils and other statutory bodies a 'duty to co-operate' in activities including the preparation of local development plans which relate to 'strategic matters'. These include the sustainable development of land which would have a significant impact on at least two planning areas.

Schedule 9 to the Localism Act 2011 contains new provisions for 'neighbourhood planning' which, in theory at least, place more decision-making power in the hands of local communities. Any 'qualifying body' (parish council or authorised neighbourhood forum) may initiate a process to require the LPA to make a neighbourhood development order. These orders grant full or outline permission for development, without the usual need for planning permission. They do not take effect unless there is a majority of support in a neighbourhood referendum. The order must also 'have regard to' national planning policy and conform to the strategic policies of the development plan. The order's compliance with these tests is checked by an independent examiner before it is put to referendum.

The Localism Act 2011 also provides for a 'community right to build', which is a type of neighbourhood development order. Community organisations can bring forward small scale development on a specific site, without the need for additional planning permission. Again, the order must conform to certain legal criteria, and must be supported by the majority of voters in a referendum. A fund to assist with the costs is run by the Homes and Communities Agency.

Another significant change in the Localism Act 2011 is the duty imposed on applicants for planning permission for certain types of development specified in a development order, to consult with people likely to be affected if permission is granted. The applicant is also under a duty to take responses into account when deciding whether to amend their proposals.

1.7 How the planning system is organised

It is important for anyone navigating the planning system, particularly if for the first time, to be aware of the role and function of the various organisations and bodies that are involved in its administration. There are essentially two tiers of administration of the planning system – central government in the shape of the Secretary of State and local government in the shape of LPAs.

Broadly, LPAs are responsible for the day-to-day operation of the system, drawing up their development plans, determining applications made to them in accordance with the development plan and taking enforcement action where necessary.

The Secretary of State oversees LPAs in two main ways. Firstly, by requiring that their development plan documents are submitted to him for independent examination, including an assessment of whether the plan is in accordance with national policy, the Secretary of State can oversee and control the LPA's vision for its area. Secondly, it is to the Secretary of State that the statutory right of appeal against a refusal of permission or against conditions imposed on a permission lies in respect of decisions taken by LPAs. In this way the Secretary of State can exercise control over individual decisions.

The other main function of the Secretary of State is to issue policy guidance for the benefit of all those involved in the planning system. With the publication recently of the *National Planning Policy Framework* (DCLG, 2012) (NPPF), the way in which the Secretary of State's planning policy is delivered has been dramatically shaken up. The main change is that the NPPF supersedes almost all of the Planning Policy Statements (PPSs) and Planning Policy Guidance notes (PPGs) which formerly constituted the planning policy framework. Over a thousand pages of policy have been condensed into 65 pages. The key policy of the NPPF is the 'presumption in favour of sustainable development'. This is addressed in more detail in Chapter 4.

These three functions of the Secretary of State, plan-making, appeals and policy guidance, are addressed in para 1.7.1 before consideration is given to the role and functions of LPAs in more detail.

1.7.1 Secretary of State

The Secretary of State with main responsibility for planning is the Secretary of State for Communities and Local Government, whose Whitehall department which assists him with his duties is called, not surprisingly, the Department for Communities and Local Government. The Secretary of State is assisted by a Minister for Planning.

Plan-making

The Secretary of State himself does not directly produce any part of the development plan. However, he currently has, and historically has always had, extensive powers to oversee LPAs' preparation of their plans and to intervene where necessary into that process to ensure that the development plan meets with his approval.

Under the old system, before the coming into effect of the PCPA 2004, the Secretary of State had specific powers, for example, to direct an LPA in London or the metropolitan areas to modify the proposals in its UDP if it appeared that the plan was unsatisfactory. In extreme cases, the Secretary of State was empowered to 'call-in' a UDP for approval by himself. Similar powers existed in non-metropolitan areas for the Secretary of State to direct modification of a Structure Plan or a Local Plan and to call-in either plan for his own approval. In this way, the Secretary of State could ultimately maintain control over plan-making even though the plan-making function was the LPAs' own responsibility.

Since 2004, LPAs' plan-making activities have been focused on the preparation of their LDF. Despite the baffling slew of newly invented terminology used to describe each part of the post-2004 plan-making regime, the Secretary of State has broadly maintained the powers he had under the old system and has arguably gained a greater level of control over LPAs' plan-making functions.

In the post-2004 system, the Secretary of State has a wide range of powers to influence an LPA's plan-making. Plan-making is necessarily a time-consuming process because of the volume of evidential analysis upon which a plan must be based which must be prepared, as well as because of the requirement for LPAs to consult before adopting a plan. The Secretary of State has powers to intervene at every stage of the process

1.7.2 Powers since 2004

Section 15 of the PCPA 2004 empowers the Secretary of State to direct the LPA to amend its local development scheme. The local development scheme is something each LPA must prepare and submit to the Secretary of State. It is essentially a list of planning documents that the LPA intends to prepare, what they are to cover and when they will be produced. It is, in effect, a project management tool for the delivery of the core strategy and other development plan documents for an area, and its purpose is to ensure that LPAs are accountable to a published timetable of work so as to minimise delay in plan-making which could delay development itself. The Secretary of State's power of direction allows him to intervene to ensure that the project of plan-making is undertaken according to his satisfaction.

The opportunity for the Secretary of State to exercise this power, however, has now largely passed since LPAs were required to prepare and submit their local development schemes to the Secretary of State by the end of March 2005. It is logical that local development schemes should have been prepared at the outset of the new system since they are intended to provide a timetable for the rest of the plan-making work to follow.

Section 20 of the PCPA 2004 requires that before adoption the LPA must submit every Development Plan Document to the Secretary of State for independent examination. One of the tests the independent examiner, who must be appointed by the Secretary of State and is in fact a Planning Inspector, is required to determine is whether the Development Plan Document is 'sound'. One of the central determinants of whether a plan is sound is whether it is consistent with national policy, i.e. policy as produced by the Secretary of State himself.

The independent examiner must make recommendations for changes to the plan and the reasons for them; the LPA is required to publish the recommendations and the reasons.

Moreover, the LPA may only adopt a Development Plan Document without changes if the independent examiner recommends that it may, or with changes if those changes have been recommended by the independent examiner. In effect, the person who ultimately determines the form of the plan to be adopted is the independent examiner who, as a result of the importance of compliance with national policy to the test of soundness is, in effect, the Secretary of State. It is in this way that, arguably, the Secretary of State has gained a greater level of control over LPAs' plan-making functions.

1.7.3 Secretary of State's intervention

In addition, the Secretary of State has the power under section 21 of the PCPA 2004 to intervene directly if he thinks that a local development document is unsatisfactory. This power allows the Secretary of State to direct that a modification is made, with reasons given; the authority must comply with the direction and the document must not be adopted unless the Secretary of State declares that he is satisfied the authority has complied. In addition, the Secretary of State has the power to direct that the document, or any part of it, is submitted to him for his approval. This is the same power of call-in that existed before 2004 and if activated the LPA plays no further part in the process of adoption of the offending plan or part of. It is a very wide power and allows the Secretary of State to take account of any matter that he thinks is relevant, regardless of whether the LPA had taken account of it.

Lastly, under section 27 of the PCPA 2004 the Secretary of State has default powers to, in essence, take over the role of the LPA and produce the plan himself if, in his view, the LPA is failing or omitting to do anything necessary in connection with plan preparation. The cost of the Secretary of State having to intervene in this way may then be claimed back by him from the relevant LPA.

In practice, the major obstacle to the Secretary of State's powers of control over plan-making both historically under the old system and under the new one, is not so much that LPAs disappear off in a direction of their own producing a plan totally at odds with, or in defiance of, the Secretary of State's policy or other requirements, it is rather that interminable delay on the part of the LPA can mean simply that no plan is produced at all or is produced very slowly. Whilst the Secretary of State does have powers to intervene directly in extreme cases, this is clearly not a power that he can exercise often as he simply does not have the resources to do so. Also, because Parliament intended that LPAs prepare their own development plans, it is consequently not a function that the Secretary of State should be performing except in exceptional circumstances.

At the time of writing, only approximately one-third of all the development plan documents identified by all LPAs' local development schemes across the country had been submitted to the Secretary of State for independent examination in accordance with section 20 of the PCPA 2004, and not even half of those submitted development plan documents were the key core strategy. This is, at the time of writing, approximately 7 years after the PCPA 2004 came into force, and illustrates well the delay that continues to bedevil the system.

1.8 Appeals

Chapter 6 deals with appeals in more detail but the focus in this chapter is on the powers of the Secretary of State in determining appeals.

Any applicant who applies to an LPA for planning permission has a statutory right of appeal to the Secretary of State against the decision of the LPA, against refusal or against the conditions imposed on a grant of permission, or against the failure of the LPA to take a decision within a prescribed period, which is known as an appeal against non-determination. This right is expressed by section 78 of the TCPA 1990. This is a central plank of the planning system and has been since the TCPA 1947, and which allows for the Secretary of State to exercise his own planning judgement and determine individual cases on appeal accordingly. In so doing, it allows for the Secretary of State to oversee the work of LPAs as well as to ensure greater consistency in decision-making.

Almost all appeals are now determined by Planning Inspectors appointed by the Secretary of State, rather than by the Secretary of State himself. Although the Secretary of State retains the power to determine an appeal himself, this power is rarely used and only in cases of significant scale, complexity or controversy. When the Secretary of State exercises his power to determine an appeal himself it is known as 'recovery' of jurisdiction because the jurisdiction which had been transferred to an Inspector by regulations is recovered by the Secretary of State himself.

It is important to note that the right of appeal is just that, a right. There is therefore no requirement for a would-be appellant to seek permission before an appeal can proceed and, subject to the discipline imposed by the costs regime to pursue his right of appeal reasonably, there is no restriction placed on an applicant appealing against an LPA's decision or non-determination.

It is equally important to note that there are no 'third party' rights of appeal. 'Third parties', in this context, means a party other than either the applicant or the LPA. As a broad generality third parties, be they neighbours, rival developers or amenity groups, are opposed to applications; they are objectors, and therefore the way in which a third party right of appeal would be most likely to be manifested would be for objectors to appeal against an LPA's grant of planning permission.

Given the level of contention that can often surround some of the most apparently straightforward applications, it can easily be seen that were third party rights of appeal allowed very many more decisions of LPAs would be the subject of appeal, and it is perhaps for this reason that the calls for third party rights of appeal has consistently been rejected by Parliament.

As discussed in para 1.8.1, for particularly controversial applications, those for which a great deal of objection may be expected, there is also a power for the Secretary of State to call-in the determination of the application himself, and in this way perhaps allow for a better expression of the extent of the objections than would by permitting third party appeals.

The Secretary of State has very broad powers in determining an appeal, pursuant to section 79 of the TCPA 1990. He may allow or dismiss the appeal, or reverse or vary any part of the LPA's decision, whether or not the appeal relates to that part; he may deal with the application as if it had been made to him in the first place. The Secretary of State is thus not constrained at all by the decision made by the LPA, and he may go so far as to refuse permission altogether in circumstances where an appeal is brought only against the LPA's imposition of a particular condition in granting permission.

1.8.1 Called in applications

In addition to being the arbiter of appeals against decisions of LPAs, or against non-determination, the Secretary of State has powers under section 77 of the TCPA 1990, to call-in an individual application for planning permission. In so doing, the Secretary of State takes the jurisdiction for the decision from the LPA and determines the application himself. It therefore differs from an appeal because the Secretary of State is taking the decision himself in the first instance. This power is exercised sparingly and essentially only in cases which are considered to be of more than local importance; this formulation of the test for the Secretary of State to exercise his power is necessarily loose but it is fair to say that it tends to be the larger, more controversial applications that are called in.

In practice, call-in operates by LPAs being required, by the Town and Country Planning (Consultation) (England) Direction 2009 to consult the Secretary of State about any application that falls within certain specified categories and which the LPA does not propose to refuse. The categories are green belt development, development outside town centres, World Heritage Site development, playing field development and flood risk area development. These categories indicate the areas of concern to the

Secretary of State and which may trigger a call-in. Once the Secretary of State has been consulted, the LPA is prevented from determining the application itself for 21 days, or until the Secretary of State notifies the LPA that he does not intend to exercise his powers under section 77 of the TCPA 1990. If the Secretary of State does decide to exercise his powers under section 77 then jurisdiction for the decision passes to him.

1.8.2 Policy guidance

The broad purpose of planning policies is to establish a framework for the making of individual decisions, the policies in effect set the criteria against which an individual application is assessed. In this way a greater uniformity and predictability of decision-making can be achieved. Without policy it would be almost impossible for any would-be applicant to gauge in advance how his application may be received; his application for permission would amount to a lottery with a decision made potentially on the whim of the decision-maker and with no continuity between decisions over time or across the country, or even across the same LPA's area.

The development plan represents the LPA's policy for planning against which it assesses individual applications, but the Secretary of State has historically produced a great deal of policy himself, although the expression of the Secretary of State's policy has been revolutionised with the publication in March 2012 of the NPPF. This is addressed in more detail in Chapter 4, but essentially there has been a massive cull of a great deal of government planning policy and its replacement with a determinedly brief single document – the NPPF.

Notwithstanding the advent of the NPPF, the purpose of the Secretary of State's policy remains the same – it is broadly to indicate how, in his judgement, particular planning matters should be dealt with. By issuing and widely publicising policy guidance, the Secretary of State can influence planning without having to intervene so often directly through appeals or call-ins of individual decisions.

It is through the promulgation and issue of policy that the Secretary of State's control of the whole planning system is perhaps most pervasive, particularly in the way in which the NPPF has been framed. This is because the Secretary of State's policies are necessarily reflected in LPAs' own development plans as a result of the requirement under the present plan-making system (section 20 of the PCPA 2004) for the development plan document to be found to be sound, and that an important element of soundness is that the document is found to be consistent with national policy. If a development plan document was found not to be consistent with national policy, it would not be sound and could not be adopted by the LPA.

Further, in determining appeals, the Secretary of State in the shape of an Inspector will have direct regard to his own policy, as he will in determining a called-in application.

It is important to be aware that policy of the Secretary of State may be directly applicable in the determination of an individual application or on appeal in the sense that if the Secretary of State's policy has been issued more recently than the LPA's adopted development plan, the Secretary of State's policy will be given more weight. This point has been emphasised with particular force in the way the NPPF is structured to come into force and is considered in Chapter 4.

Historically, i.e. prior to the NPPF, the Secretary of State's policy was expressed either through a Circular or through a PPS. PPSs were the more recent form of policy expression and were issued in place of their predecessor, PPGs. PPSs were gradually superseding PPGs although both have now been largely superseded by the NPPF. There remain, however, some PPSs which have survived the publication of the NPPF, and it is useful to be aware of the existence of those that have been replaced by the NPPF since they and PPGs featured so prominently in all planners' lives for so long.

Circulars are issued sequentially simply with a number which indicates where in the sequence a particular Circular was issued by a particular government department in that year, so for example the Circular about costs awards in appeals and other planning procedures is known as CLG Circular 03/2009: *Costs Awards in Appeals and Other Planning Proceedings* (TSO, 2009), being the 3rd Circular issued by the Department for Communities and Local Government (the department that has the main responsibility for planning), and the Circular explaining changes to the regulations for dwelling houses and houses in multiple occupation made in 2010 is known as CLG Circular 08/2010: *Changes to Planning Regulations for Dwellinghouses and Houses in Multiple Occupation* (TSO, 2010). Generally, Circulars have not been replaced by the NPPF.

PPSs, and before them PPGs, simply had a number and a title which described what they addressed. Perhaps the most well known PPG was PPG2: *Green Belts* (TSO, 1995) which, before it was replaced by the NPPF, had been in force since 1995. Other examples include, PPS3: *Housing* (TSO, 2006 (1st edn), 2010 (2nd and 3rd edns), 2011 (4th edn)), PPS4: *Planning for Sustainable Economic Growth* (TSO, 2009) and PPG8: *Telecommunications* (TSO, 2001).

1.9 Local planning authorities

1.9.1 What is the local planning authority?

Section 1 of the TCPA 1990 states which authorities comprise the LPAs in England. In order to understand how the LPAs are arranged, it is necessary to know a little of how local government itself is arranged, and more pertinently how it has frequently been rearranged since the Second World War.

Moving from the most urban to the most rural parts of the country, in London the LPA is the respective London borough of which there are 33. The London boroughs are long established, having been created in the local government reorganisation of 1965.

In the metropolitan areas, i.e. the great industrial conurbations of Greater Manchester, Merseyside, South Yorkshire, Tyne and Wear, West Midlands and West Yorkshire, the LPA is the metropolitan district council within that conurbation. Greater Manchester is comprised of ten metropolitan districts, Merseyside five, South Yorkshire four, Tyne and Wear five, West Midlands seven and West Yorkshire five. For example, Bury, Gateshead, Kirklees, Rotherham, Sandwell and Sefton are all metropolitan district councils. The metropolitan districts were created by the local government reorganisation that came into effect in 1974 which also established the metropolitan county councils, one for each of the six industrial conurbations; those county councils, however, were abolished in 1986 at the same time as the Greater London Council.

Each of these LPAs, London boroughs and the metropolitan district councils is a unitary authority. This is not a phrase used to describe planning functions in particular but one associated with local government generally, and it simply means that the unitary local authority performs all local government functions within its area; there is no sharing of functions between authorities at different levels, such as between a district council and a county council. What this means, therefore, in planning terms is that in London and the metropolitan districts each authority has, since 1986 when the Greater London Council and the metropolitan county councils were abolished, produced a UDP. As its name suggests, a UDP is a unitary plan combining the strategic and local planning functions in one document.

Areas outside London and the industrial conurbations described above are known as non-metropolitan areas, and local government in these areas in England is either two-tier with a district council and a county council, or increasingly there is in place a more recently created unitary authority. In these areas, unitary authorities were created during the 1990s or in 2009. There are now 55 of these more recently created unitary authorities, for example East Riding of Yorkshire, Medway, Shropshire or Stockton-on-Tees.

Where there remains a two-tier structure the planning function is shared between the district planning authority and the county planning authority. Where there is a unitary authority it is treated in planning terms as both a county council and a district council, the effect of which is that the unitary authority is the LPA.

In addition to the above, there are a number of exceptions, areas where some of the planning functions are carried out by a different body such as, for example, a National Park Planning Board, the Broads Authority for the Norfolk Broads, an urban development corporation, an enterprise zone, a housing action area trust area or an urban regeneration area.

The key task of LPAs is deciding whether to grant planning permission for development in their areas. The circumstances in which planning permission is required are explained in Chapter 2.

1.9.2 What are the functions of the local planning authority?

In broad terms, the work of the LPA is to prepare plans, both strategic and local and to exercise development control functions. That is, to set out the vision for its area in the development plan and then to control the grant of planning permission in accordance with the aim of achieving the vision as set out in the plan. Whilst these functions may be expressed very briefly as here, in fact these tasks form the great bulk of the day-to-day planning work undertaken by the LPA.

There are certain powers relating to planning which London boroughs enjoy which other authorities elsewhere do not. For example the power to order the stopping up or diversion of a highway if it is satisfied that it is necessary to do so in order to enable development to be carried out, under section 247 of the TCPA 1990; outside London this power may be exercised by the Secretary of State rather than the LPA.

1.9.3 Plan-making

In London and the metropolitan areas since 1986, under the old system of plan-making – that is before the coming into effect of the PCPA 2004 – each London borough and metropolitan district produced its own UDP, which combined strategic and local planning within the same document.

In non-metropolitan areas before the coming into force of the PCPA 2004, there remained a two-tier system of plan-making with, generally, the county council preparing the more strategic structure plan and the district council preparing the more detailed local plan. There were and remain also 'county matters', generally the preparation of plans for minerals and for waste, which are specifically the preserve of the county council.

In areas where a new unitary authority was created during the 1990s, the Secretary of State had power to order that a UDP be prepared but instead has usually preferred for the two-tier system to continue, with the structure plan maintained by joint working between the authorities that have responsibility for the area formerly administered by the county council.

The PCPA 2004 substantially changed the way in which plans are made and this is reflected in the division of functions between different sorts of authorities. The strategic planning function of structure plans prepared by county councils was abolished and with it the bulk of county councils' role in plan-making. Under the PCPA 2004 the strategic element of plan-making was set out in the Regional Spatial Strategy but this new (in 2004) level of the planning hierarchy has itself recently been abolished, except in London.

Responsibility for drawing up the newly conceived development plan in the shape of the LDF passed to the LPA as defined in section 37 of the PCPA 2004. This definition of an LPA reflects these changes, so as to include district councils, London borough councils, metropolitan councils or county councils in relation to any area in England for which there is no district council (this is a reference to the relatively rare unitary county authority, for example Herefordshire).

Where there remains a two-tier system with a county council and a district council in place, it is the district council which is charged with preparing the development plan and the county council is explicitly restricted to county matters (section 14 of the PCPA 2004). The PCPA 2004 does, however, allow for county councils to retain some role in assisting district councils in plan preparation through joint working if directed to by the Secretary of State, but the main effect of the PCPA 2004 was to remove the bulk of plan-making powers from the county councils, which had been performing this role more or less since 1947.

It is important always to be aware of the status of a development plan in any particular area and the timetable for its replacement. Because of the time that it necessarily takes an LPA to prepare a development plan, under the old or the new (i.e. pre- or post-2004) systems, there is inevitably a period when the former plan remains in force but its replacement is in the course of preparation and will be publicly available; in other words, there is an overlap between plans. There will come a time when the replacement plan is adopted and the former plan ceases to have any effect. Adoption occurs on a particular date with the consequence that a plan that has been in the public domain for many years can cease to have any effect literally overnight. Relying on a plan that has ceased to have effect is to be avoided, but equally so is relying on a draft replacement plan that has not yet been adopted.

1.9.4 Development management

There are many ways in which planning permission may be granted but by far the most common is by an LPA on an application. That is, somebody wishing to undertake development applies to the LPA for permission to do so. The process by which the LPA determines the application, decides whether or not to grant permission, is known as development management, formerly development control. This fundamental transaction lies at the heart of the system of planning control in this country and provides the bulk of the planning work undertaken by LPAs. Section 57 of the TCPA 1990 provides that planning permission is required for development of land, and section 58 confirms that it may be granted by the LPA.

The LPA which has responsibility for determining an application is that within which the site of the proposed development lies, and is as follows:

- in London – the London borough;
- in metropolitan areas – the metropolitan district council;
- in areas with a unitary authority outside London and the metropolitan areas – the council of that unitary authority; and
- in areas where there remains a two-tier system with a district council and a county council – the district council unless the application concerns a county matter, in which case it is the county council.

2 The Requirement for Planning Permission

Planning permission is permission given by the LPA for development to be carried out on land. It is required by law for a wide range of building, engineering and mining projects both large and small, as well as changes to the way land or buildings are used. It is also known as planning consent.

The phrases 'planning control', 'development control' or, more recently, 'development management' mean the power of planning authorities to limit and shape development in their areas, by granting or refusing planning permission. If a development is said to be 'outside planning control' it means that planning permission is not required and the planning authority has no say in whether or how the development is carried out.

Failure to obtain planning permission before carrying out works to or changing the use of land is not a criminal offence in itself. However, in many cases the LPA will take enforcement action against unauthorised development which can lead to a criminal conviction and a substantial fine. In addition to its planning enforcement powers, the LPA is empowered to regulate the development of listed buildings and development in conservation areas. These are discussed in Chapter 5, paras 5.9 and 5.10.

2.1 Key concepts

Planning permission is required for development on land. There are many exceptions to the requirement. As this chapter sets out, even if permission is required under statute it is important to be aware that there may be exemptions under the Town and Country Planning (General Permitted Development) Order 1995 (SI 1995/418) (GPDO) as amended.

The GPDO is not infrequently updated and new categories of 'permitted development' (for which planning permission is not required) are added.

The main statutory scheme governing the requirement for planning permission is set out in Part III of the TCPA 1990 and the GPDO. Section 55 of the TCPA 1990 defines development as:

> the carrying out of building, engineering, mining or other operations in, on, over or under land, or the making of any material change in the use of any buildings or other land.

There are two types of development for the purposes of planning control:

(a) operational development;

(b) material change of use.

The two are often closely linked – in many cases building works (operational development) are needed to facilitate a change in the way a building is used.

2.2 What is operational development?

'Operational development' is a term used to cover the types of development referred to in the first part of section 55 of the TCPA 1990 – building, engineering, mining and other operations in, on, over or under land.

These types of operational development are defined to some extent within the Act but there is often room for interpretation. Where definitions exist they are to be found in section 336 of the TCPA 1990.

2.2.1 Building operations requiring planning permission

All building operations which are not permitted development will require planning permission. However, not all built structures are 'buildings' for the purposes of the TCPA 1990.

What is a 'building'?

Planning permission is required under the TCPA 1990 for 'building operations'. A building is not defined in the Act but section 336(1) provides that it 'includes any structure or erection and any part of a building, as so defined, but does not include plant or machinery comprised in a building'. The requirement for planning permission applies to any part of the building as well as to the whole.

In some cases it is obvious that a structure is a building, for example a dwelling house or a supermarket. In other cases, such as structures which are temporary or can be dismantled easily, it is less clear.

The question of whether or not a structure is a building in planning terms is a 'matter of fact and degree'. This is a recurring piece of jargon in the context of planning, meaning there are no hard and fast rules and all the circumstances must be looked at before making a decision. However, in deciding whether a structure is a building there are three main factors to be taken into account:

1. *Size*: a structure does not have to be large to be a building, but will usually be something constructed on site rather than brought on to it. In *Buckinghamshire County Council v Callingham* [1952] 2 QB 515, a model railway and village standing no more than 4 feet high was held to be 'development' for the purposes of the TCPA 1947, notwithstanding its small size.

2. *Permanence*: a building is usually intended to be in place for some time and is not easily dismantled. Examples of structures that the courts have found not to be buildings are fairground swing boats and touring caravans. However, a structure which is temporary in the sense that it remains in place for some time but is eventually removed and subsequently re-erected in the same place is likely to require planning permission; for example, a marquee which is in place for several months out of every year, as was the case in *Skerritts of Nottingham Ltd v Secretary of State for the Environment, Transport and the Regions (No 2)* [2000] JPL 1025.

3. *Physical attachment to the land*: while not a deciding factor on its own, the degree of attachment to the land can make all the difference if the other factors do not provide a clear answer. In *R (Hall Hunter Partnership) v First Secretary of State* [2006] EWHC 3482 (Admin), the High Court upheld the Planning Inspector's decision that agricultural polytunnels constructed by machinery on top of legs penetrating 1 metre into the ground constituted operational development due in part to their degree of attachment to the land.

Building operations

A building operation is work to land of the sort which would normally be carried out by a builder, for example creating an extension or remodelling a roof. Most types of building operation require planning permission. Carrying out structural alterations to a building also usually requires planning permission. Partial demolition is also a building operation and requires planning permission, though total demolition of some buildings is exempt from planning control.

Section 55(1A) of the TCPA 1990 provides that building operations include:

(a) demolition of buildings;

(b) rebuilding;

(c) structural alterations of or additions to buildings; and

(d) other alterations normally undertaken by a person carrying on business as a builder

2.2.2 Demolition

Planning control over the demolition of buildings is a relatively complex area despite the fact that demolition is clearly defined as a 'building operation' in section 55(1A)(a) of the TCPA 1990. It is wrong to assume that planning permission is required for all types of demolition. Section 55(1A) must be read together with two key provisions:

- Class A, Part 31 of Schedule 2 to the GPDO, which provides that planning permission is not required for the demolition of buildings.

- Circular 10/95: *Planning Controls over Demolition* (DOE, 1995) and the Town and Country Planning (Demolition – Description of Buildings) Direction 1995 at Annex A to Circular 19/95 (as amended in 2011).

The Direction, which came into force on 3 June 1995, in its original form listed a number of descriptions of buildings that were not development for the purposes of the TCPA 1990, with the effect that demolition of these types of building did not require planning permission. They were:

(a) listed buildings;

(b) buildings in conservation areas;

(c) scheduled monuments;

(d) any buildings other than a dwelling house or a building adjoining a dwelling house;

(e) any building greater than 50 cubic metres when measured externally;

(f) the whole or part of any gate, fence, wall or other means of enclosure unless in a conservation area.

Therefore, planning permission was required:

1. *Outside conservation areas*: for the demolition of dwelling houses and buildings.

2. *Within conservation areas*: for the demolition of gates, fences, walls or other means of enclosure.

However, following a legal challenge by an historic building campaign group, the Court of Appeal held that exceptions (a) to (d) were unlawful (*Save Britain's Heritage v Secretary of State for Communities and Local Government* [2011] EWCA Civ 344). The impact of the judgment is that demolition of a listed building, a building in a conservation area, a scheduled monument or building that is not a dwelling house or adjoining a dwelling house, now qualifies as development, bringing the treatment of building demolition in line with works to residential buildings generally (see Chapter 5, para 5.9).

Permitted development rights still apply to these types of demolition but an application must be made to the LPA in advance to find out whether prior approval of the method of demolition, and any proposed restoration of the site, is needed (see para 2.2.3).

The Court of Appeal also followed the judgment of the European Court of Justice in Case C-50/09 *Commission v Ireland*, 3 March 2011, which concluded that demolition works fall within the scope of Directive 85/337/EEC, known as the Environmental Impact Assessment Directive. Where demolition works are likely to have a significant effect on the environment, the LPA is required to issue a screening opinion as to whether an Environmental Impact Assessment (EIA) is required.

Note that in addition to planning permission, consent for works to listed buildings, in conservation areas and to scheduled monuments is required where relevant.

Partial demolition

The exceptions listed in the GPDO only apply in the case of complete demolition. Partial demolition is generally regarded as development because it is a structural alteration and so comes within section 55(1A)(c) of the TCPA 1990.

2.2.3 Permitted demolition of dwelling houses (Class A)

Class A of Part 31 of the GPDO grants permitted development rights for the demolition of dwelling houses and buildings attached to them, subject to a number of conditions. Paragraph A.1 of Part 31 contains the single exception to this right – demolition is not permitted if the building has become unsafe due to the action or neglect of anyone with an interest in the land on which the building stands, and it is practicable to 'secure safety or health by works of repair or works of temporary support'. The legislation is intended to prevent landowners from benefitting from letting buildings fall into disrepair.

However, deemed permission for demolition is subject to a number of conditions. If the demolition is immediately necessary in the interests of safety and health, then the developer must provide a written explanation to the authority as soon as reasonably practicable. Where demolition is not immediately necessary, the developer must apply to the local authority to find out whether prior approval will be required. The developer must provide a written description of the proposed development and a statement that notice has been posted on the site as required. The basic requirement is that a notice must be displayed on site for not less than 21 days within the 28-day period following determination by the authority. However, it is advisable to check the precise requirements in paragraph A2.

There are time limits on when demolition can be started. The developer must wait until one of the following has occurred:

(a) the authority has indicated that no prior approval is required;

(b) where prior approval was required, it has been given;

(c) 28 days have expired since the authority received the application and it has either not made a decision or not communicated that decision to the developer.

Demolition must be carried out within 5 years of the approval, or of the application if approval is not required.

There are also limits on how the demolition can be carried out. If prior approval was not required, demolition must still be carried out in accordance with the details the developer submitted with the application. Where approval has been given, demolition must be carried out in accordance with the approved details.

2.3 Permission not required for internal works

Planning is generally concerned with impact on shared or public space, so works which affect only the interior of a building do not 'materially' affect the external appearance of the building and do not require planning permission. This is addressed at para 2.3.1. However, it is crucial to bear in mind when carrying out works to a listed building that consent is required for changes to the interior even when planning permission is not.

This exception, which appears at section 55(2)(a) of the TCPA 1990, applies to a 'building' not to a unit of occupation. So, for example, a large shopping mall is considered to be a single building even though it comprises a number of units which may be separately occupied.

Therefore, alterations to the exterior of a shop within a mall will not be an alteration to the exterior of the building itself and so do not require planning permission.

2.3.1 What is a 'material impact on the exterior' of a building?

Again, this is a question of fact and degree. Some operations like painting a building a different colour or putting up cladding would require planning permission if they were not subject to exceptions under the GPDO. Any visual impact must be 'material', i.e. visible from normal vantage points whether on the street or from neighbouring dwellings. The materiality of the change has to be assessed against the whole of the building and not just the part that has been altered. For example changing the position of a small window at the back of a large house is unlikely to be material, but creating a bay window on a previously flat fronted terrace house will be material (in addition to being an alteration to its structure).

2.3.2 Basements

Planning permission is often required for the creation of additional space underground, i.e. a basement or cellar, where major works are involved. However, the change of existing basement space to living space will not require permission unless the nature of the use is significantly changed, or a light well is added.

2.3.3 Driveways

The construction of a driveway or pedestrian path between a building and the street is an 'engineering operation' under section section 336(1) of the TCPA 1990, being the 'formation or laying out of means of access to a highway'.

2.3.4 Exceptions to the internal works rule

There are two important exceptions to the rule that planning control does not apply to works which affect only the interior of a building. They are:

1. *Listed buildings*: even though planning permission is not required for works to the interior, listed building consent is required. It is a criminal offence to carry out works to the interior of a listed building without consent, in any way that would affect its character as a building of special architectural or historic interest. There is

clearly an element of subjective judgment involved in determining whether the works would affect this character, but in the majority of cases it is advisable to obtain consent prior to commencing work.

2. *Works incidental to a change of use which requires planning permission*: if a planning enforcement notice is issued against an unauthorised change of use, it may require incidental operational works to be removed even if they only affect the interior of the building. For example, an enforcement notice issued against the unauthorised conversion of a dwelling house into flats can require the removal of internal partitions and staircases which facilitate the unlawful use.

2.3.5 Engineering operations

There is no statutory definition of 'engineering operation' besides the interpretation in section 336 of the TCPA 1990, which states that it includes 'the formation or laying out of means of access to highways'. Access in this context can be by foot or vehicle, and includes both public and private access. The courts have interpreted 'engineering operation' to mean an operation that would generally be supervised by an engineer (including a traffic engineer), even if it was not in fact so supervised.

Exceptions

Again, there are exceptions to the rule – engineering operations do not always require planning permission. The exceptions are:

1. Local highway authorities have statutory authority to carry out works of maintenance and improvement within the boundary of a road or incidental works adjoining the boundary, and do not require planning permission.

2. Local authorities or statutory undertakers (e.g. electricity and water suppliers) do not require planning permission to carry out works of inspection or repair to sewers, water mains, pipes, cables or other apparatus.

2.3.6 Mining operations

Planning permission is generally required for mining operations, which again are not defined in the TCPA 1990. Section 55(4) sets out the operations which come under this heading, and include the removal of 'material of any description' from a mineral-working deposit (i.e. the deposit of minerals remaining after extraction), the removal of material from a deposit of pulverised fuel as or other furnace ash or clinker. Also included is the extraction of minerals from a disused railway embankment.

Exception for exploratory works

Exploratory works to determine the presence of minerals in land is likely to be on a small scale with minimal impact and therefore outside the scope of planning control altogether. Further, Schedule 22 of Part 2 to the GPDO grants planning permission on conditions for mineral exploration operations lasting up to 28 days and more extensive operations lasting up to 4 months.

2.4 What is a material change of use?

The second type of development for which planning permission is generally required is material change of use. A 'change of use' is a change in the kind of use land is put to, for example a change from a shop to an office. It will not always be 'material' and the question of whether or not it is material involves a degree of subjective judgment.

There are four main issues to consider when looking at material changes of use:

1. The physical extent of the planning unit.
2. The current use of the planning unit.
3. The rights which flowed from the previous use.
4. Whether any change is material.

2.4.1 The planning unit

The fundamental concept in understanding material change of use is that of the 'planning unit'. The planning unit is the appropriate physical area against which to assess the degree or 'materiality' of change brought about by a different use. It often, but not always, corresponds to the unit of occupation or land ownership. A large site in the same unit of occupation or ownership may contain a number of different planning units; for example, a large out of town supermarket may occupy a site including the supermarket itself, extensive parking space, a petrol station and other associated uses. Depending on the circumstances, some or all of those may constitute a separate planning unit within the main unit of occupation.

Burdle v Secretary of State for the Environment [1972] 3 All ER 240 remains the classic judgment on determining the correct planning unit. There are three key tests:

1. Is it possible to recognise a single main purpose to the occupier's use of land?

    If the answer is 'yes', and any other activities on the land are incidental or ancillary to that main use, then the whole unit of occupation should be taken as the planning unit.

2. If it is not possible to recognise a single main use (plus ancillary uses) but rather a number of different uses which are not confined within physically separate and distinct areas on the site and may fluctuate in intensity over time, then this is called a 'composite' use and the whole unit of occupation should still be taken as the planning unit.

3. If in the single unit of occupation there are two or more physically separate and distinct areas occupied for substantially different and unrelated purposes, then each area should be considered as a separate planning unit.

2.4.2 Types of use

The concepts of main use and ancillary uses are central to being able to determine the extent of the planning unit. The main use of a site is often quite easy to categorise, for example a school, a church or a supermarket. The Town and Country Planning (Use Classes) Order 1987 (Use Classes Order 1987) (as amended) identifies numerous types of use and frequently a use will fit neatly into one of these categories.

2.4.3 Ancillary uses

'Ancillary' uses are uses which are connected but subordinate to the main use. For example, customer car parking at a supermarket is an ancillary use, but a public car park next to a supermarket will not be ancillary even if the land is in the same ownership because its purpose is not incidental to that of the supermarket. Rather, it has a separate and distinct purpose of its own as a car park.

A single planning unit may, and often does, have a single main use together with incidental or ancillary uses. The ancillary uses are essentially subordinate to the main use. For example, the site may contain a main building used as a shop, and a smaller building used for administration connected to the main retail use.

The test of ancillary status is one of fact and degree. Uses which are not in the normal course of events ancillary to the main use are likely to require planning permission. For example, in the case of *Harrods v Secretary of State for the Environment, Transport and the Regions and the Royal Borough of Kensington and Chelsea* [2002] JPL 1258, the Court of Appeal refused to overturn the Secretary of State's decision not to grant a certificate of lawful development for a helicopter landing pad on top of Harrods store in London. This was despite the fact that the pad was intended solely for the use by the owner of the shop in connection with his work in directing its operations. The Inspector had found that the use was not in the 'ordinary and reasonable' practice of the management of department stores, and could not therefore be an ancillary use.

The character of the planning unit's use is determined by the main use, not the ancillary uses. In the case of a school, for example, there may be a main school building on site together with a number of maintenance buildings, a car park for teachers and recreational facilities. As long as these other uses remain ancillary, or subordinate, to the main use of the land as a school, then the owner or occupier of the land can change the way the buildings and land within the site are used (e.g. convert sports changing rooms to a classroom). However, if the school opened up a sports club on the site to members of the public, then this may be a material change of use creating a separate planning unit and requiring planning permission, because it would no longer be subordinate to the main school use.

In summary, planning permission is not required for:

1. The addition of ancillary uses to the main use of a site.
2. Changing one ancillary use for another, or moving the location of ancillary uses around a site.

Planning permission is, however, required when:

1. A previously ancillary use becomes a primary use.
2. A new use takes place which is not ancillary to the main use.

2.4.4 Composite uses

If more than one separate use is carried out on the site but there is no identifiable main use, and no physical separation between the uses, the unit is described as being in 'composite use'. Planning permission is not required for some fluctuations in the level of intensity of each particular use. Care must be taken to distinguish between sites in composite use and sites which have a main use together with ancillary uses connected to it. The cessation of an ancillary use will not require planning permission.

Where a site is in composite use, the 'mere cessation' of one element of use will not amount to a material change of use of the site overall. However, if one use is allowed to absorb the whole of the site to the exclusion of all others, then it is a matter of fact and degree whether a material change of use has taken place. In *Wipperman & Bucking v Barking LBC* (1996) 17 P & CR 225, the appellant's site had been used for two unrelated purposes – the storage of building materials and car-breaking. The car-breaking use ceased and the storage of building materials took over the whole site. The council issued an enforcement notice. The High Court held that the uses were not ancillary to one another; the cessation of the car-breaking activity and the exclusive use of the site for storage purposes amounted to a material change.

2.4.5 Physical separation

Physical distance between two sites in the same occupation will usually mean that there are two separate planning units. However, if a building is erected on a previously unbuilt part of the site, it may appear as if there are now two distinct areas (i.e. one with the building and one without). Unless there is a material physical separation between the two, then the new building may be used for the same purposes as the rest of the site or for use ancillary to the main use.

In *Duffy v Secretary of State for the Environment* [1981] JPL 811, premises formerly used as accommodation for staff working in an hotel 150 yards distant were held not to be part of the same planning unit as the hotel.

2.4.6 Functional separation

Separation between use types leading to the creation of a new, separate planning unit can happen if a former ancillary use becomes a separate use altogether. An important case explaining this principle is *Williams v Minister of Housing and Local Government* (1965) 18 P & CR 514.

The High Court held that in determining whether a material change of use had taken place, the proper unit to be considered was the whole of the land rather than the particular part of it containing the new use. The land concerned was a nursery garden containing a shed, from which fruit and vegetables grown in the garden were sold, ancillary to the main agricultural use. The appellant made improvements to the building and began to sell produce not grown in the garden. The High Court found that:

> there is clearly, from a planning point of view, a significant difference in character between a use which involves selling the produce of the land itself, and a use which involves importing goods from elsewhere for sale. All sorts of

planning considerations may arise which render one activity appropriate and desirable in a neighbourhood and the other activity quite unsuitable.

There was no great difference in the character of the use of the shop taken in isolation (i.e. it was still selling the same amount of produce), but it was no longer ancillary to the nursery garden because produce from outside the site was being sold – a functional separation had taken place.

2.4.7 What rights flow from the current use?

It is important to bear in mind that the extent of rights flowing from an existing use depends on whether or not planning permission was granted. If it was, then the use is limited to what is specified in the permission (and to any changes permitted within the GPDO).

Where permission is granted for erecting building (operational development), but no use is specified in the planning permission, then the permitted use is that for which the building was designed (see section 75 of the TCPA 1990).

2.5 When is change material?

Having identified the planning unit and ascertained that a change of use has taken place, the next matter to determine is whether or not the change is material. The change must be considered against the 'baseline' of the existing use. Assessing materiality of change is not always straightforward. In the simplest cases there will be a change of use of the whole planning unit from one class of use to an entirely different class (e.g. school to factory), but change is often more often gradual and incremental. Changes which have no planning impact (i.e. no impact on the amenity of neighbouring occupiers or the public in general) are likely to be *de minimis* and outside the scope of planning control. A change in ownership or occupation is unlikely to be material.

2.5.1 Intensification of use as a material change

'Intensification of use' means a perceptible increase in the use of a planning unit for its existing purpose. For example, weekend market stalls in a car park may become permanent, attracting customers 7 days a week. There will be a corresponding increase in traffic, noise and reliance on public services, such as refuse collection.

Intensification is not in itself a material change of use requiring planning permission. To qualify as a development and trigger the requirement for planning permission, the intensification must amount to a material change in the character of the use. This can be determined by looking for material increases in the land-use impact of the change, i.e. increases in noise or traffic, or reliance on public services.

2.5.2 Intensification of use within the Use Classes Order 1987

A distinction must be made between intensification of a use which falls in to a category within the Use Classes Order 1987 (as amended), e.g. A1 (retail) or A2 (financial and professional services) and use which does not. If the use falls within a Class of the Order then intensification of that use will not amount to a material change unless the character of the use is altered.

In *Brooks and Burton Ltd v Secretary of State for the Environment & Anor* [1977] 1 WLR 1294, the Court of Appeal held that intensification of a light industrial use would not, without any change in the nature of the operations, amount to a material change of use. The appellant's site had planning permission for light industrial use (Class IV of the then, 1972, Use Classes Order). The site was originally occupied by a building in which concrete blocks were made. The blocks were then moved outside for drying. The appellant bought the site and substantially increased its operations. The manufacture of blocks outside began and this lead to increased noise and complaints. The Court of Appeal rejected the Inspector's finding that the intensification of use amounted to a material change. The land outside the building had been used for block-making operations and so the whole site was a 'general industrial building' for the purposes of the Order and there was no change in the character of the use. However, the Court observed that:

> We have no doubt that intensification of use can be a material change of use. Whether or not it is depends on the degree of intensification. Matters of degree are for the Secretary of State to decide.

2.5.3 Intensification of use not within the Use Classes Order 1987

In the case of uses outside the Use Classes Order 1987, intensification leading to a material land use impact may (but will not in all cases) amount to a material change of use which requires planning permission. The case of *R (Childs) v First Secretary of State* [2006] JPL 1326 is a useful illustration of this principle. This case concerned the terms of a lawful development certificate (considered at para 2.9) which had been granted for use of a field as a caravan site; a use outside the Use Classes Order 1987.

The number of caravans was limited by the certificate. The question for the Court was whether an increase in the number of caravans on site from four to eight or more would amount to a material change of use. As the certificate contained a limit on the number of caravans, a material increase would take the use outside the scope of the certificate and planning permission would be required.

However, the Court observed that had the certificate not contained this limit, an increase in number of caravans would not have amounted to a material change in use, even though there would have been a material planning impact, the reason being that under the certificate the use of the planning unit as a caravan site would not have been limited to any particular intensity. It is therefore important for LPAs to be clear about the intensity of use permitted by lawful development certificates and clearly state limits if any are intended.

2.5.4 Intensification of ancillary uses

Ancillary uses can be intensified without planning permission, but not beyond the point where the ancillary link is broken and a separate use is created. The point at which this break occurs is a matter of fact and degree.

2.5.5 Flat conversions

Section 55(3)(a) of the TCPA 1990 provides that the use of a single dwelling house as two or more 'separate dwelling houses' requires planning permission. The term 'dwelling house' may be somewhat confusing as it includes types of accommodation not thought of as houses, namely flats and maisonettes. So, if a single dwelling house (a house, flat or other self-contained unit of residential accommodation) is subdivided for use as two or more units, then planning permission will be needed.

Conversions are usually created by physically subdividing the existing house or flat, for example by putting in new partition walls and doors. However, sometimes a material change of use may take place without this kind of work being carried out. In *Wakelin v Secretary of State for the Environment & Anor* (1983) 46 P & CR 214, planning permission had been granted for the construction of separate residential accommodation in the grounds of a large house, on condition that it was only occupied by people closely associated with the main house. The Court of Appeal confirmed that the house and the lodge were one planning unit to begin with. Use of the lodge by people not associated with the main house would equate to use 'as two or more dwellings of a building previously used as a single dwelling house' and therefore a material change of use.

2.5.6 Changes within use classes

Under section 55(2)(f) of the TCPA 1990, buildings or other land in use for a purpose specified the Use Classes Order 1987 may be used for a purpose within the same class without planning permission.

The Schedule to the Use Classes Order 1987 consists of four parts, A, B, C and D, each listing a number of use classes.

In summary, these are:

Class A1	Retail use.
Class A2	Financial and professional services.
Class A3	Sale of food or drink.
Class A4	Public house or other drinking establishment.
Class A5	Hot food takeaway.
Class B1	Office (other than A2) or light industrial use.
Class B2	General industrial use (not B1).
Class B8	Use for storage or as a distribution centre.
Class C1	Hotel, hostel or boarding house – no significant element of care provided for residents.
Class C2	Care homes, hospitals, residential schools, colleges or training centres.
Class C2A	Secure residential accommodation, for example young offenders institution.
Class C3	Dwelling house – single household.
Class C4	House in multiple occupation (up to six residents).
Class D1	Non-residential institution.
Class D2	Assembly and leisure.

2.5.7 Sub-classes of use classes

The majority of these main use classes contain sub-classes. For example, Class D2 (assembly and leisure) contains: (a) cinema; (b) concert hall; (c) bingo hall; (d) dance hall, etc. The effect of section 55(2)(f) of the TCPA 1990 is that a change of use within the use class, for example from cinema to bingo hall, does not require planning permission.

Note that changes of use from one use class to another do not automatically require planning permission. The change of use must still be material.

Some changes from one use class to a different use class are explicitly permitted under the Use Classes Order 1987. An example is change of use to A1 (shop) from A3 (restaurant/cafe), A4 (drinking establishment) or A5 (hot food takeaway) under Class A, Part 3 of Schedule 2 to the GPDO. The rationale is that the change is likely to reduce the planning impact of the use and therefore permission is not required. Part 3 contains the full list of permitted changes from one use class to another. Note that the majority of such changes are not reversible without permission.

Sui generis use

Uses which do not fall into one of the classes under the Use Classes Order 1987 are described as *sui generis* (of their own type). Article 3(6) contains a non-exclusive list of sui generis uses, including: theatre; launderette; taxi business; hostel; nightclub. So, change between sui generis uses, or between a sui generis use and one falling into a use class, will require planning permission unless the change is not material in light of the considerations discussed in para 2.5.

2.6 Exceptions to the need for planning permission for material change of use

There are three main exceptions to the requirement of planning permission for material changes of use. These are:

1. Use of land within the curtilage of a dwelling house.
2. Use of agricultural and forestry land and buildings.
3. Changes of use permitted by the Use Classes Order 1987 (as amended).

2.6.1 Incidental uses with the curtilage of a dwelling house

Section 55(2) of the TCPA 1990 provides that the use of any buildings or land within the curtilage of a dwelling house for any purpose incidental to 'the enjoyment of the dwelling house as such' is not development. This is a concession to residential occupiers, allowing them to use their gardens in an ordinary way.

This exception does not extend to the construction of sheds or other buildings within the dwelling house because this is operational development and not use. However, this sort of minor operational development may come within the terms of the GPDO.

What is the curtilage?

The curtilage of any building, not just a dwelling house, is usually a small area of land immediately surrounding it. Ancillary buildings may fall within the curtilage of a dwelling house, and intimacy of association rather than size is the main identifying characteristic. The curtilage of an ordinary dwelling house would include the front and rear gardens and any driveway. It includes land which serves the dwelling house in a necessary manner; land which is not so used will fall outside the curtilage, for example a rough wooded area beyond well-kept gardens.

2.6.2 Use incidental to the enjoyment of the dwelling house

To be exempt under section 55(2) of the TCPA 1990, the use of the building or land within the curtilage must be incidental to the enjoyment of the dwelling house as such, i.e. it must be connected to ordinary residential use. There is an element of reasonableness and the section is not intended to pander to the 'unrestrained whim' of the occupier. Examples of uses which have been found not to be incidental are:

- stock car racing;
- parking of commercial vehicles;
- keeping unusually large numbers of dogs (see *Wallington v Secretary of State for Wales* [1991] JPL 942);
- keeping a replica Spitfire in front of the house.

2.6.3 Use of agricultural land

Section 55(2)(f) of the TCPA 1990 exempts the use of land for the purposes of agriculture or forestry (including afforestation) and the use of any buildings on land used in these ways, from the definition of development.

'Agriculture' is defined in section 336(1) of the TCPA 1990 as including:

> horticulture, fruit growing, seed growing, dairy farming, the breeding and keeping of livestock (including any creature kept for the production of food, wool, skins or fur, or for the purpose of its use in the farming of land), the use of land as grazing land, meadow land, osier land, market gardens and

nursery grounds, and the use of land for woodlands where that use is ancillary to the farming of land for other agricultural purposes

Changes of use within these descriptions, and changes of use from non-agricultural to agricultural land do not require planning permission.

Keeping horses for the farming of land (e.g. ploughing or pulling) does not, without anything further, require planning permission. However, keeping horses other than for the purpose of farming the land is not an excluded use and requires planning permission (see *Belmont Farm Ltd v The Minister of Housing and Local Government* (1962) 13 P & CR 417).

2.6.4 Ancillary use of agricultural land

The question often arises whether selling agricultural produce on agricultural land is an ancillary use not requiring a separate planning permission. Generally, if only produce from the farm itself is sold, then this will not constitute development. However, if the produce is processed first, then the ancillary link may be severed and planning permission is required (see *Williams v Minister of Housing and Local Government* (1965) 18 P & CR 514, discussed at para 2.4.6).

2.7 Permitted development rights

Permitted development rights are a creature of statute. Numerous types of building works and changes of use are thereby not development for the purposes of planning control.

2.7.1 Town and Country Planning (General Permitted Development) Order 1995

'Permitted development' means development that would otherwise require planning permission but, due to the operation of the GPDO, does not. Therefore, it is important always to check the GPDO to determine whether or not planning permission is actually required.

Under article 3 of the GPDO, permission is granted for the classes of development described in Schedule 2 to the Order. Additional approval is required for development sited in special nature conservation areas under the Conservation (Natural Habitats &c) Regulations 1994 (SI 1994/2716).

The Town and Country Planning (Environmental Impact Assessment) Regulations 2011 (SI 2011/1824) restrict the operation of the GPDO. Under regulation 3(1), development listed in Schedule 1 or Schedule 2 of the Regulations is not permitted without a screening opinion or direction (subject to certain exceptions, e.g. development for national defence purposes). Examples of Schedule 1 development are crude oil refineries and nuclear power plants. Schedule 2 development includes intensive agriculture and intensive livestock installations.

2.7.2 Directions under article 4 of the Town and Country Planning (General Permitted Development) Order 1995

In some circumstances, the GPDO can be rendered inapplicable. Under article 4(1), the Secretary of State or LPA may direct that permitted development rights in any part of Schedule 2 (apart from Part 22 Class B and Part 32 Class C, which both relate to mineral workings – see, also, article 7) do not apply to certain areas of land. Article 4 directions are often made in conservation areas and rural locations.

If the direction is made by the LPA, the Secretary of State's permission is required, except where the direction relates to a listed building or development within its curtilage or in the case of development in Parts 1 to 4 and Part 31 of Schedule 2 to the GPDO. In the latter case, the direction can only be made if in the opinion of the authority the development would be prejudicial to the proper planning of its area or constitute a threat to its amenities. Directions made by the LPA in these circumstances can only remain in force for 6 months unless confirmed under article 5(9) within the 6-month period.

An order under article 4 of the GPDO does not prevent development altogether but means that development requires planning permission. Statutory undertakers carrying out the types of maintenance work listed in article 4(3) are exempt.

2.7.3 Schedule 1 to the Town and Country Planning (General Permitted Development) Order 1995

Schedule 1 to the GPDO lists the parts of England and Wales to which stricter controls on permitted development rights apply.

- *Article 1(5) land*: National Parks, conservation areas and Areas of Outstanding Natural Beauty. Stricter development tolerances apply under Part 1 (householder development), Part 8 (industrial development), Part 17 (statutory undertakers), Parts 24 and 25 (telecommunications).

- *Article 1(6) land*: National Parks and land in specified rural areas.

2.7.4 Schedule 2 to the Town and Country Planning (General Permitted Development) Order 1995

Schedule 2 to the GPDO lists the different types (which are designated into Parts in the Schedule) and classes of permitted development.

The most commonly referred to are Parts 1 and 2. Part 1 permits 'development within the curtilage of a dwelling house' namely enlargements of and additions to dwelling houses within defined limits (also known as 'development tolerances'). This includes roof enlargements and rear extensions.

Part 2 permits minor operations, for example painting the exterior of a building and constructing an access to the highway.

Part 3 of the Schedule sets out permitted changes of use from one use class to another. The underlying purpose is to permit changes which are likely to have a better impact in planning terms so in the majority of cases the change is 'one way only'. One adverse consequence for landowners is that rights may be inadvertently lost. For example, a change from general industrial use to light industrial use is permitted, but planning permission is usually required to revert to the original use.

Part 4 grants permission for various temporary buildings and uses. Temporary buildings which facilitate a lawful use of land are permitted under Class A of Part 4. In *North Cornwall DC v Secretary of State for the Environment, Transport and the Regions* [2003] 1 PLR 28, the High Court held that the provision of a temporary structure on the forecourt of a building, enabling retail use to carry on inside, was permitted development within this Class.

Temporary uses for 'any purpose' are granted permission under Class B of Part 4. This applies only to open land and not to buildings or land in the curtilage of a building. 'Temporary' means for not more than 28 days in all cases apart from markets and car/motorcycle racing, in which case the period of use is limited to 14 days. In practice, this means that there can be numerous changes of use within the permitted period as long as the 28 days (or 14 days, as the case may be) are not exceeded. Exceptions set out in paragraph B.1 are use of land for a caravan site or for advertising, and in the case of Sites of Special Scientific Interest, use for clay pigeon shooting, war games or car and motorcycle racing.

The remaining parts of Schedule 2 cover such diverse uses as caravan sites (Part 5), aviation development (Part 18) and mineral exploration (Part 22).

2.8 Simplified planning zones and enterprise zone schemes

Simplified planning zone (SPZ) schemes under section 82 of the TCPA 1990 are another mechanism by which planning permission is deemed to be granted. The purpose of SPZs is to allow LPAs to deregulate planning in their areas by granting general planning permission for development in a particular area. SPZs cannot apply to certain protected categories of land including National Parks, conservation areas and green belt land (section 87(1) of the TCPA 1990). They are subject to a time limit of 10 years.

Under section 88 of the TCPA 1990 enterprise zones designated by Order under the Local Government, Planning and Land Act 1980 have the effect of granting planning permission for the types of development specified in the Order. The scheme may be subject to conditions and limitations.

Development falling within Schedule 1 or Schedule 2 to the Town and Country Planning (Environmental Impact Assessment) (England and Wales) Regulations 1999 (SI 1999/293) (known as EIA development) is not automatically granted permission if it is located within an SPZ adopted or approved after 14 March 1999.

2.9 Certificates of lawfulness

The LPA is empowered to issue certificates confirming that a particular use or development is lawful and, therefore, immune from enforcement action.

2.9.1 Certificates of lawfulness for proposed use or development

Where there is uncertainty about the lawfulness of a proposed development or use of land, an application may be made to the LPA under section 192 of the TCPA 1990. If the local authority is provided with information 'satisfying it' that the use or development would be lawful if begun at the time of the application, the certificate – a certificate of lawfulness for proposed use or development (CLOPUD) – will be granted. The certificate is usually referred to as a 'lawful development certificate'. An application can be made by anyone, not just the owner or occupier of the land in question.

A proposed use may be lawful if, for example, it is not a material change of use. Proposed development may be lawful if it does not constitute development for the purposes of section 55 of the TCPA 1990 and no planning permission is required.

Guidance on the approach authorities should adopt is provided in paragraph 8.2 of Annex 9 to Circular 10/97: *Enforcing planning control – legislative provisions and procedural requirements* (1997) (Circular 10/97):

> In making their decision on an application under section 192, the LPA will ask themselves the hypothetical question – 'If this proposed change of use had occurred, or if this proposed operation had commenced, on the application date, would it have been lawful for planning purposes?' In doing so, they will not only consider whether the proposal would involve 'development' requiring an application for planning permission, but whether it would involve a breach of any existing condition or limitation imposed on a grant of planning permission which has been acted upon, and which therefore constrains what can be done on the land

Once a certificate is issued, then it is conclusively presumed that the use or development is lawful, unless there is a material change before the use is instituted or the operations begun in any of the matters relevant to determining lawfulness. So, for example, if after grant of a certificate permitted development rights are removed by a direction under article 4 of the GPDO before the development has begun, the certificate will no longer be valid.

2.9.2 No 'development'

Annex 8 to Circular 10/97 explains that development or other activity on land is lawful for planning purposes if it is within one of the following categories and does not involve a failure to comply with a condition or limitation subject to which planning permission has been granted:

1. it is not within the definition of development in section 55(1) and (1A) of the TCPA 1990 (this might be because it is so insignificant that it can be disregarded – a *de minimis* operation, use or activity – or because it involves a change of use which is not, as a matter of fact and degree, materially different, for planning purposes, from a previous lawful use of land); or

2. it is specifically excluded from the definition of development by section 55(2) of the TCPA 1990 (e.g. a use of land for the purpose of agriculture); or

3. it is within the definition of development in section 55 of the TCPA 1990, but is exempted from the need for planning permission by the provisions of section 57; or

4. it benefits from an extant grant of planning permission under Part III of the TCPA 1990 (or the equivalent Parts of preceding Acts); or

5. it benefits from a general planning permission granted by the GPDO, or by a simplified planning zone or enterprise zone scheme; or

6. it benefits from deemed planning permission, whether under section 90 of the TCPA 1990 or by virtue of compliance with the requirements of an effective enforcement notice; or

7. it took place before 1 July 1948 (the 'appointed day', see Country Planning Act 1947); or

8. it is development by or on behalf of the Crown; or

9. the time for taking enforcement action has expired.

2.9.3 Certificates of lawfulness for existing use or development

Issued pursuant to section 191 of the TCPA 1990, a certificate of lawfulness for existing use or development (CLEUD) certifies that the use or development on land at the date of the certificate is lawful. This is conclusively presumed in the same way as the lawfulness of a proposed use certified under section 192. As under section 192, the applicant must provide the authority with sufficient evidence to satisfy it that the existing use is lawful. The burden of proof is on the applicant, and the standard of proof is the balance of probabilities, not the higher criminal standard of proof. In practice, applications for CLEUDS are more common than applications for CLOPUDs.

CLEUDs are particularly useful where, for example, a single dwelling house has been subdivided into flats without planning permission. Any prospective buyer of such a converted dwelling would be well advised not to proceed until the certificate has been obtained.

Section 191(2) of the TCPA 1990 provides that existing use or development is lawful if:

> (a) no enforcement action may then be taken in respect of them (whether because they did not involve development or require planning permission or because the time for enforcement action has expired or for any other reason); and
>
> (b) they do not constitute a contravention of any of the requirements of any enforcement notice then in force.

2.9.4 Immunity from enforcement action

A lawful development certificate will be issued in cases where the use or development has become lawful over time and it is too late for the LPA to take enforcement action by issuing a planning enforcement notice under section 172 of the TCPA 1990. Section 171B contains the time limits for taking enforcement action. Note that operational development becomes immune from enforcement action 4 years after the substantial date of completion, and changes of use after 10 years. For example, a change of use from a single dwelling house to self-contained flats becomes immune from enforcement action after 4 years and not 10 years. The rationale behind this is external operational development is more visible than internal change of use, and likely to be brought to the LPA's attention in a shorter time frame. If 10 years have passed without a change of use being reported, it is unlikely to have had any material planning impact and enforcement is not expedient.

Determining when operational development is substantially complete or when a material change of use took place is a 'matter of fact and degree' and so not always straightforward.

The basic principle was set out by the House of Lords in *Sage v Secretary of State for the Environment, Transport and the Regions* [2003] UKHL 22. The intended character and use of the finished building is the determining factor. Per Lord Hope of Craighead at [7]:

> If it is shown that all the developer intended to do was to erect a folly, such as a building which looks from a distance like a complete building – a mock temple or a make-believe fort, for example – but was always meant to be incomplete, then one must take the building when he has finished with it as it stands. It would be wrong to treat it as having a character which the person who erected it never intended it to have. But if it is shown that he has stopped short of what he contemplated and intended when he began the development, the building as it stands can properly be treated as an uncompleted building

Paragraph 8.15 of Annex 8 to Circular 10/97 sets out the applicable 'balance of probabilities' test. The evidence provided by the applicant has to be sufficiently precise and unambiguous to meet the test, and not undermined by the authority's own contradictory evidence. LPAs will often check council tax and business rates records, for example, to determine whether they corroborate the applicant's evidence, but as the Circular emphasises:

> If the LPA have no evidence of their own, or from others, to contradict or otherwise make the applicant's version of events less than probable, there is no good reason to refuse the application, provided the applicant's evidence

alone is sufficiently precise and unambiguous to justify the grant of a certificate 'on the balance of probability'

2.8.5 Failure to comply with a planning condition

Development in breach of a condition on which planning permission has been granted may also be lawful in the circumstances set out in section 191(3) of the TCPA 1990 if:

> (a) the time for taking enforcement action in respect of the failure has then expired; and
>
> (b) it does not constitute a contravention of any of the requirements of any enforcement notice or breach of condition notice then in force.

By way of example, planning permission for a warehouse (operational development) may be granted with a condition that raw materials are not stored on the forecourt (use). If this unauthorised use takes place for more than 10 years, no enforcement action can be taken. A lawful development certificate can then be issued for the development or change of use which constituted the breach of condition.

2.8.6 Revocation

Under section 193(7) of the TCPA 1990 the LPA may revoke a lawful development certificate if, on the application, a statement was made which was 'false in a material particular' or any material information was withheld. The LPA must be able to identify precisely the statement which is said to be false. Notice must be given to the owner and occupier of the land before the certificate is revoked, so that they have the opportunity to make representations.

There is no provision for appeal against revocation, but there is nothing to prevent the landowner from applying for a further certificate.

2.8.7 Appeal against refusal

Applicants can appeal against the LPA's refusal to grant a certificate, or failure to determine an application within 8 weeks, under section 195. The appeal will be determined by a Planning Inspector, and allowed if the authority's refusal is 'not well founded' or in the case of non-determination, if refusal would not have been well founded.

The process of applying for planning permission is explained in Chapter 3.

3 Applying for Planning Permission

There are many different sorts of planning permission that may be applied for. This chapter focuses on the most common forms of application – for outline and for full consent – as well as touching on applications for retrospective consent and for conservation area consent and listed building consent. The less common forms of application (e.g. for removal or variation of a condition, works to trees or prior notification for agricultural development) are not addressed here.

This chapter focuses on the process of applying for permission. Chapter 4 then addresses how LPAs go about determining applications.

It is important to note that an application for planning permission on a particular piece of land may be made by anyone; the application does not have to be made by the person who owns the land or has any other interest in it. The owner's interest is protected by a requirement that he or she is notified of the application by the applicant. The requirement for an applicant to notify the owner of the land to which the application relates, or a tenant, is in article 11 of the Town and Country Planning (Development Management Procedure) (England) Order 2010 (SI 2010/2184) (DMPO), while under article 12 the applicant must certify on the application form itself that the requirement of article 11 has been satisfied – that notice of the application has been given to the owner or tenant of the land affected.

The certificates are in fact incorporated into the standard form for making a planning application, discussed further at para 3.5.

In practice, most applications are either made by or on behalf of the owner or in accordance with an agreement about transfer of the land should the permission be granted.

3.1 Pre-application consultation with the local planning authority

Before formerly applying for planning consent it may be wise for a would-be applicant to discuss his proposal in advance with the LPA.

This is particularly so for larger schemes which have the potential to affect more people and therefore to attract more objections.

There is not yet (see para 3.2) a requirement for any prospective applicant to discuss with the LPA in advance what development he or she proposes with the planning application, but there can be some advantage in getting an early indication of how a proposal is likely to be received by the LPA, and in ascertaining what particular information the LPA is likely to want to have included in any subsequent planning application.

Commonly, what may be ascertained by the applicant through early engagement with the LPA is how a particular policy or policies are likely to be interpreted by the LPA, or if there are elements of what is proposed that are less or more likely to meet with the approval either of officers or members of the LPA, for example the appearance of a proposed building and how it affects the setting of a nearby listed building, or the change of use of a building that is currently in a use that may be particularly valued by the community.

A thorough and frank pre-application exchange can result in better applications that are more 'accurate' in the sense that they meet the LPA's expectations as well as those of the applicant; this can result in the saving of a great deal of the applicant's and the LPA's time and money by avoiding the expense of preparing an application that is refused and which may subsequently have to be appealed.

That said, how LPAs handle pre-application discussions varies widely across the country. Some LPAs are quite business-like about it and charge for the service; others are more informal and may not charge. However, the key thing to remember is that the LPA officer will make absolutely clear that any advice cannot be and will not be binding on the LPA's formal decision on any application subsequently made; pre-application discussions are intended to be a useful service for applicants that indicate the LPA's general views about a proposal and must not be treated as anything more. This is particularly so if the decision about whether to grant consent is not one that is to be taken by officers themselves under delegated powers but is to be taken by elected members. An officer could in good faith indicate his or her support for a proposed development only for elected members, quite legitimately, to take a different view in determining the application proper.

For large developments which are likely to excite more interest locally, the determination of planning applications can very often become political in that arguments for and against a particular proposal may be reflected in the differing stance of local politicians and their public utterances. This has had the potential to cause difficulties for local elected representatives who would be expected to reflect those constituents' views in relation to the proposal which may well be strongly held. However, as members of the LPA's planning committee, the politicians would have to show that they had not pre-determined the application, i.e. to have approached the decision about whether to grant planning permission with a closed mind. The Localism Act 2011 recognises and addresses this problem and in section 25 states that a decision-maker is not to be taken to have had a closed mind just because he or she had previously indicated what view he or she would or might take.

There is now quite a well established branch of the public affairs industry involved in running consultations for developers in advance of the submission of a planning application, particularly for larger schemes. At their best they allow for a genuine reflection of local residents' wishes to emerge in the eventual scheme; at their worst they are seen as an attempt to provide political 'cover' for an unpopular scheme.

3.2 Statutory pre-application consultation

However, a clear distinction must be made between pre-application consultation as described in para 3.1, which is and has long been essentially good practice for the putative applicant, and the new statutory provision in section 61W of the TCPA 1990, introduced by the Localism Act 2011, which places a statutory obligation on a person proposing to make a planning application to consult the majority of the persons who live at, or otherwise occupy, premises in the vicinity of the land the subject of the proposed development. Section 61W is supplemented by s 61X which places a duty on the applicant who has consulted under section 61W to have regard to any responses received.

It should be noted that section 61W is not (at the time of writing) fully in force.

3.3 Outline permission

An applicant may apply for outline permission for a proposed building if he or she wishes simply to get an indication in principle of the acceptability of the development before he or she embarks on the expense and trouble of devising and submitting detailed plans for it. The application for outline permission requires considerably less detail about the proposed building than an application for full permission does. The scheme of outline permission is a means for a developer to 'test the water' before committing more resources. If granted, an outline permission is always subject to a condition which requires the submission in due course of 'reserved matters', i.e. the detailed plans that were not submitted with the application for outline permission but would have been had the application been for full permission. This is reflected in the definitions of both 'outline planning permission' and 'reserved matters' in article 2 of the DMPO:

> 'outline planning permission' means a planning permission for the erection of a building, which is granted subject to a condition requiring the subsequent approval of the local planning authority with respect to one or more reserved matters;
>
> ...
>
> 'reserved matters' in relation to an outline planning permission, or an application for such permission, means any of the following matters in respect of which details have not been given in the application—
>
> (a) access;
>
> (b) appearance;
>
> (c) landscaping;
>
> (d) layout; and
>
> (e) scale, within the upper and lower limit for the height, width and length of each building stated in the application for planning permission in accordance with article 4(4) [that is the application for outline planning permission];

The LPA is not obliged to determine the application for outline application if, in its opinion, more detail is needed; that detail may be demanded by the LPA before the application is determined (article 4(2) of the DMPO). This power is usually used in circumstances where it is particularly important for the LPA to understand how a building would actually appear, for example if development is proposed in a conservation area. There is a right of appeal against, in effect, the LPA's non-determination of the outline application by requiring more detail, pursuant to article 33(1) and 33(2)(d)(ii) of the DMPO.

3.4 Expiry of outline permissions

All outline permissions must expire after a certain period. This is to prevent the whole planning system from becoming jammed with old consents which would, and in the past often did, make determination of the lawful use of a piece of land very difficult because of the myriad overlapping stale consents. There is a similar provision in respect of full consents in section 91 of the TCPA 1990.

The requirement for outline consents to expire is effected by section 92 of the TCPA 1990 which automatically imposes a condition on all outline consents that any application for reserved matters must be made within 3 years of the grant of the outline consent and the development itself must begin within 2 years of the final approval of the reserved matters. An LPA has the power under section 92 to impose its own time limits in respect of both approval of reserved matters and beginning the development itself, longer or shorter, but if the LPA does not do so then the statutory periods will be deemed to have been imposed by condition. The LPA may also specify separate periods for separate parts of a development.

In practice, LPAs very often routinely expressly impose a condition in accordance with the time limits specified in section 92 of the TCPA 1990.

3.5 Application for full permission

This section focuses on applications for planning permission (sometimes called 'full permission or consent' to distinguish them from outline consent). The application is, essentially, the process by which the applicant provides all the information the LPA needs to determine whether to grant permission.

The Planning Portal (www.planningportal.gov.uk) is a website which is described as the UK government's 'online planning and building regulations resource for England and Wales'. It is a very valuable source of information about all planning matters and as well as providing useful information for all users of the planning system and allowing for planning applications to be made online.

An application for permission (article 6 of the DMPO) must be in writing and on the standard application form as published by the Secretary of State, or a form substantially the same. The standard application form is available online for applicants to fill in via the Planning Portal website and although described as the standard application form (singular), in fact, there are a number of different versions of it which are generated automatically when details are filled in by the applicant online. So, for example, there are different versions of the form generated for applications for householder consents, for listed building or conservation area consents.

The particulars specified in the form must be provided and it must be accompanied by a plan which identifies the land to which the application relates and any other plans, drawings or information necessary to describe the development.

3.6 Information requirements

CLG *Guidance on information requirement and validation* (DCLG, 2010) (CLG Guidance) interprets the minimum requirement for a plan in the DMPO as comprising both a location plan and site plan. The location plan in essence shows where the application site is by showing its location in the context of the surrounding area. It should be based on an up-to-date map, at a suitable scale to indicate precisely where the application site can be found, if possible scaled to fit onto a single sheet of either A3 or A4. The area the subject of the application should be edged with a red line, which should include all the land necessary to carry out the proposed development including, for example, land required for access from the highway, visibility splays, landscaping, car parking and open areas around the buildings.

The long established convention that any other land outside but near to the application site owned by the applicant should be edged with a blue line on the location plan is also set out in the CLG Guidance.

3.7 Site plan

A site plan shows more detail about the application site itself. It must be scaled (usually at a larger scale than the location plan because it shows the smaller area of the site itself rather than the site in its context), orientated north and show the proposed development in relation to the site boundaries and other existing boundaries on the site with written dimensions including those to the boundaries.

The site plan must also show all of the following unless they would neither influence nor be affected by the proposed development – all buildings, roads and footpaths on land adjoining the site including access arrangements; all public rights of way crossing or adjoining the site; the position of all trees on the site and on adjacent land; the extent and type of any hard surfacing; and boundary treatment including walls or fencing where proposed.

These are the minimum requirements for plans and, in practice, a scheme of any size will be accompanied by full plans showing floor plans, elevations, sections and roof plans as relevant to the development. These further plans would usually be required on a local list, discussed at para 3.9.1.

3.8 Particulars

The particulars required by the form itself comprise the basic information about the applicant and his or her agent and about the proposal itself. There are 30 separate sections of the form, which gives an indication of the extent and range of the information that is sought, although it should be noted that the standard application form is designed to be used for almost all sorts of planning applications and not all sections will be relevant to every application.

Information is required about the proposed development, for example, description, site area, pedestrian and vehicle access, parking, waste storage and collection, materials, foul sewage, flood risk, existing use, proposed number of residential units or non-residential floor-space. Information is also sought about the applicant and agent, if there is one, as well as if there has been pre-application advice sought and if the applicant is related to either a member or employee of the LPA.

Lastly, the application form contains the ownership certificates which confirm that either the applicant is the owner of the land or, if not, that the owner has been notified of the application, or that it has not been possible to notify the owner (which may occur if the land to which the application relates is not registered, for instance), together with an agricultural land declaration. This confirms either that none of the land to which the application relates is an agricultural holding or that if the land or part of it is an agricultural holding then any tenant of the land has been notified of the application.

3.9 Design and access statements

Extensive though the information sought on the planning application form may seem, it is the bare minimum.

This is because most applications, full or outline, for developments comprising a new building of any size are required also to be accompanied by a Design and Access Statement (DAS), as defined by article 8 of the DMPO. Essentially, this document is a statement of the design principles and concepts that have been applied to the development and of how issues relating to access to the development have been dealt with.

Article 8 of the DMPO describes the contents of a DAS as follows:

(3) A design and access statement shall—

(a) explain the design principles and concepts that have been applied to the following aspects of the development—

(i) amount;

(ii) layout;

(iii) scale;

(iv) landscaping; and

(v) appearance; and

(b) demonstrate the steps taken to appraise the context of the development and how the design of the development takes that context into account in relation to its proposed use.

(4) A design and access statement shall also—

(a) explain the policy adopted as to access, and how policies relating to access in relevant local development documents have been taken into account;

(b) state what, if any, consultation has been undertaken on issues relating to access to the development and what account has been taken of the outcome of any such consultation; and

(c) explain—

(i) how any specific issues which might affect access to the development have been addressed;

(ii) how prospective users will be able to gain access to the development from the existing transport network;

(iii) why the main points of access to the site and the layout of access routes within the site have been chosen; and

(iv) how features which ensure access to the development will be maintained.

The DAS is an important document. Its purpose, according to the CLG Guidance, is to encourage good design which is said to play a fundamental role in the achievement of sustainable development. The DAS should ensure that the proposals are based on a thoughtful design process and a sustainable approach that shows the merit of the scheme and how it relates to the existing setting; this to assist the LPA in understanding the analysis that has underpinned the design and how it has led to the development of the scheme. The explanation of the design component of a scheme should focus on the amount, layout, scale, landscaping and appearance of the development. This, in turn, helps negotiations and decision-making and should lead to an improvement in the quality, sustainability and 'inclusiveness' of the development. The DAS is also intended to allow local communities, access or amenity groups and other stakeholders to involve themselves more directly in planning.

That said, the CLG Guidance emphasises that DASs must be proportionate to the complexity of the application and need not be long.

3.9.1 Local area requirements

Further to the requirement for a DAS, by section 62(3) of the TCPA 1990 the LPA may require such additional particulars to accompany a planning application as it thinks necessary, with evidence in support. This is often known as a local list. In order for the LPA to be able to require these additional particulars and evidence, details of what is required must be published on the LPA's website.

There is no statutory limit to what additional information an LPA may seek and whilst practice varies across the country, there is scope for even the most humble planning application to require a colossal amount of information and evidence in support. Some may regard this as an overbearing and heavy-handed bureaucratic imposition; others as a way of ensuring better informed and speedier decision-making.

The CLG Guidance has sought to exert a measure of control by urging those LPAs that did not have a local list (as at 6 April 2010) to prepare one and for those that did at that time to review them; this exercise was expected to have been completed by the end of 2010. The CLG Guidance proposed that this preparation/review of local lists exercise was done in accordance with five principles – necessity, precision, proportionality, fitness for purpose and assistance.

Overall, in respect of the amount and nature of the information that must be provided with an application for planning consent, the regulations and the CLG Guidance seek to strike a balance between furnishing LPAs with all that they require to make a properly informed decision and burdening the applicant with the obligation of producing all manner of extraneous material at great expense.

3.9.2 Fees

A fee is payable to the LPA to which an application is submitted, which is intended to cover the administrative cost to the LPA of receiving and determining the application (Town and Country Planning (Fees for Applications and Deemed Applications) Regulations 1989 (SI 1989/193)). The fee is calculated in accordance with the size of the development proposed, whether outline or full, so the larger the development the larger the fee subject to a maximum. For example currently, for an application for full permission for the erection of 50 or fewer dwelling houses the fee is £330 per dwelling house; for schemes over 50 dwelling houses the fee is £16,464 plus an additional £84 for every dwelling house over 50, subject to a maximum of £250,000. For the erection of buildings other than dwelling houses the fee is determined by the extent of gross floor space. For outline permissions for dwelling houses or other buildings, where the detail of the actual dwellings or buildings is not known, the fee is determined by the application site area.

There is no fee for applications that concern the alteration or extension of an existing dwelling house, for operations within the curtilage of the dwelling house, for works to facilitate the access of disabled persons to a public building or for permitted development.

Further, a fee is not payable in a number of circumstances where, broadly, the same applicant makes an application for the same development on the same site within 12 months of an application that had previously been either granted, withdrawn before being determined, refused by the LPA or on appeal, or appealed to the Secretary of State. This is a concession to the applicant that allows him to re-apply quickly for the same scheme on the basis that the additional work that this creates for the LPA is covered by the initial fee. Whether or not the concession applies in any particular case, however, is a matter for the LPA.

3.9.3 Validation

When the LPA has received all the information that is required to be submitted in support of the planning application described at paras 3.5–3.9.2 and the requisite fee, it must send an acknowledgment of receipt of the application to the applicant (article 10 of the DMPO). This is an important stage in the process known as 'validation'. It is important because the time within which the LPA must determine the application, either 8 weeks or 13 weeks for a major application, starts to run from the date of validation. If, after the end of the relevant period a valid application has not been determined by the LPA, the applicant has the right of appeal to the Secretary of State for non-determination of the application.

The LPA is not obliged to validate an application if it does not believe it has received all the information which must be provided by the applicant. Discretion lies with the LPA in deciding whether or not to validate, and the CLG Guidance urges LPAs not to take too mechanistic an approach to this question.

It is good practice, which is generally observed, that upon receipt of inadequate information from an applicant, the LPA will write to him or her setting out precisely what it is that is missing, so giving the applicant an opportunity to remedy the deficiency, rather than the LPA simply refusing to validate the application.

Importantly, upon receipt of an application, the LPA may conclude that the description of the development in the application is not accurate. In these circumstances the LPA is able to substitute its own description of the development, or otherwise amend the description, but it may not do so without first consulting with the applicant.

3.9.4 Publicity

Once an application has been validated, the LPA is obliged to publicise it before determining the application. Publicity is an important part of the decision-making process. It makes the details of the application known to those most likely to be affected by it and consequently most likely to express a view about what is proposed. This stage of the process is rooted in the nationalisation of the right of individuals to develop land – in order for the LPA to take a decision that is in accordance with the public interest, it is necessary that the public is made aware of a proposed development so that they have the opportunity to comment. For this reason, it is not overstating the case to say that the requirement for publicity about planning applications makes a crucial contribution towards the planning system being democratically accountable and inclusive.

Because it has such an important role in the overall scheme of the planning system, the requirements for publicising a planning application are precisely controlled. The requirements, which fall on the LPA, are set out in article 13 of the DMPO. Article 13 broadly distinguishes between three categories of development for the purposes of publicity – so-called 'paragraph 2' development, major development and other development.

Paragraph 2 development is that which requires an Environmental Impact Assessment (EIA) application accompanied by an EIA statement, does not accord with the development plan in force for the area or would affect a public right of way.

EIA is largely outside the scope of this book but is a requirement for certain types of development and requires brief mention here. EIA is a procedure that seeks to make information available about the likely environmental effects of a major development before planning permission is granted. The procedure is governed by its own set of regulations – the EIA Regulations – which are structured in such a way that planning permission for a development to which the Regulations apply must not be granted unless the decision-maker has taken the environmental information into account. The aim is to safeguard the environment from unwitting damage or destruction by larger developments.

EIAs originally derive from an EEC Directive dating from 1985 which was subsequently transposed into UK law by Regulations which have been subject to a number of subsequent amendments. The EIA legislation and case law is very complex and is the topic of many specialist texts in its own right to which the reader is referred.

The publicity requirements for paragraph 2 applications are the placing of at least one site notice on or near the land to which the application relates, which must remain for not less than 21 days, and the publication of a notice in a newspaper circulating in the locality in which the land to which the application relates is situated.

'Major development' is defined for the purposes of the DMPO and consequently for the publicity requirements in article 2, as development involving any one or more of the following:

> (a) the winning and working of minerals or the use of land for mineral-working deposits;
>
> (b) waste development;
>
> (c) the provision of dwellinghouses where—
>
>> (i) the number of dwellinghouses to be provided is 10 or more; or
>>
>> (ii) the development is to be carried out on a site having an area of 0.5 hectares or more and it is not known whether the development falls within sub-paragraph (c)(i);
>
> (d) the provision of a building or buildings where the floor space to be created by the development is 1,000 square metres or more; or
>
> (e) development carried out on a site having an area of 1 hectare or more;

For applications for major developments that are not paragraph 2 applications, the publicity requirements are that there is a notice displayed on or near the land to which the application relates for not less than 21 days or any adjoining owner or occupier must be served by notice, and there must be a notice published in a local paper circulating in the locality in which the land to which the application relates is situated.

For applications that are neither paragraph 2 applications nor for major development, the publicity requirements are that there is a notice displayed on or near to the land to which the application relates for not less than 21 days or that any adjoining owner or occupier be served with a notice. There is no requirement for a notice in a local newspaper.

It can be seen that broadly, the larger or more significant or contentious the development that is being applied for, the more publicity is required.

In addition to the above, all applications are required to be publicised on the LPA's website by way of publication of the following information:

(a) the address or location of the proposed development;
(b) a description of the proposed development;
(c) the date by which any representation about the application must be made, which shall not be before the last day of the period of 14 days beginning with the date on which the information is published;
(d) where and when the application may be inspected;
(e) how representations may be made about the application; and
(f) in the case of householder applications in the event of an appeal that proceeds by way of the expedited procedure, any representations made about the application will be passed to the Secretary of State and there will be no opportunity to make further representation.

3.9.5 Register of planning applications

There are other separate means by which the public may become aware of planning applications that have been made. Each LPA must maintain a register of every application made in its area (section 69 of the TCPA 1990 and article 36 of the DMPO) and there is, as part of their plan-making responsibilities, an obligation on all LPAs to publish a Statement of Community Involvement written in consultation with the public, which should explain how the LPA will engage the public throughout the planning process. Most LPAs' planning committee meetings are open to the public and the papers for these meetings are usually publicly available.

However, it is through the methods specified in article 13 of the DMPO that applications are actively publicised before they have been determined. This allows anyone the opportunity to make his or her views known in advance of the decision being made.

The methods specified in article 13 of the DMPO are deliberately easy to understand and open to all (even those without a computer). Anyone walking past a site for which an application has been made should be able to see the notice put up on or near the land (the notices are often laminated to protect them from the weather), and anyone scanning the local paper should easily see a notice published in it.

The most recent consultation on publicity, which in fact recommended the making of web publication of applications by LPAs obligatory, proposed removing the requirement for LPAs to publish notices in local papers. This was rejected by the government on the basis that many public and community groups rely on newspaper notices and that there is no good alternative arrangement that can be rolled out.

Having made such detailed provisions for publicity to be given to planning applications by LPAs, it is not surprising that they are then required (by article 28 of the DMPO) to take any resultant representations into account when determining the application.

3.10 Consultation

Whereas publicity about an application, as described in para 3.9.4, is broadly intended to elicit the views of interested parties such as neighbours (adjoining owners or occupiers) and the general public – essentially for reasons of democratic accountability, so that these peoples' views may be represented in the decision-making process – the consultation obligations placed on an LPA have a different purpose.

Consultation is intended to ensure that the LPA which is to determine an application gets expert advice from the organisations with the expertise relevant to the application in hand. For it to be meaningful it is important that LPAs provide enough information about the proposed development to the organisation it is consulting for that organisation to make sense of what is proposed and to give it sufficient time within which to consider how to respond. It is also important that the LPA takes into account any advice it receives as a result of the consultation when determining the application.

3.10.1 Statutory consultees

The DMPO (article 16) requires an LPA to consult a prescribed list of authorities or persons relevant to a particular application before permission is granted.

The list of consultees is extensive and clearly not all are relevant to every application. It is for the LPA to decide which consultees must be consulted for any particular application.

For example, if development is likely to affect land in a National Park, the National Park authority must be consulted or if development is likely to result in a material increase in the volume or a material change in the character of traffic entering or leaving a classified road or proposed highway, then the local highway authority must be consulted. Similarly, for any development involving the formation, laying out or alteration of any means of access to a highway (other than trunk road – for a trunk road the Secretary of State for Transport must be consulted) or the construction of a highway or private means of access to premises affording access to a road in relation to which a toll order is in place, the local highway authority concerned must be consulted and in the case of a road subject to a concession, the concessionaire.

The Environment Agency is required to be consulted on a number of common sorts of development, for example those involving the use of land for the deposit of refuse or waste, for development other than minor development (as defined) which is to be carried out on land in an area within Flood Zone 2 or Flood Zone 3 or in an area within Flood Zone 1 which has critical drainage problems and which has been notified for the purpose of this provision to the LPA by the Environment Agency. Flood Zones 1 to 3 are also all defined (in the notes to Schedule 5 to the DMPO), with the likelihood of sea or river flooding greater in Flood Zone 3 and less in Flood Zone 1.

Other common consultees include the Historic Buildings and Monuments Commission for England, which is required to be consulted for development involving demolition, in whole or part, or the material alteration of a listed building in Greater London, and Natural England must be consulted about development likely to affect a site of special scientific interest.

There are also some less common consultees. The Theatres Trust, for instance, which must be consulted about development involving land on which there is a theatre.

In addition to the statutory consultees set out in the DMPO which LPAs must consult, there are also a number of bodies which LPAs are encouraged to consult.

3.10.2 Time limits

Article 29 of the DMPO requires that where a valid application has been received by the LPA (that is when the application is validated), it shall give the applicant notice of its decision or determination or notice that the application has been referred to the Secretary of State within 13 weeks for an application for a major development, and within 8 weeks for an application that is not a major application or it may extend the period for determination in agreement with the applicant. The definition of major development is in article 2 of the DMPO and is the same as is referred to in the provisions about publicity, set out in para 3.9.4.

The time limits are a very important aspect of the process of the planning system. Since they are easily measured they are often used as a crude indicator of LPAs' efficiency in determining the applications they receive, sometimes with funding consequences for the LPA. Whilst, in general, it is important that all LPAs are subject to the same widely known time limits so that applicants regardless of where they are in the country know what they can expect and slow LPAs are thereby encouraged to speed up, sometimes the tyranny of a crude indicator can have unintended consequences. There may be circumstances where rather than invest a few more days or weeks in negotiation with an applicant to produce an application that is acceptable, an LPA may simply refuse a scheme that is very largely acceptable so as to comply with the 8-week or 13-week time limit. This is wasteful of resources, particularly if an appeal is made against the refusal and does nothing to foster good relations between LPAs and developers.

3.11 Written notice of decision

The form of the notice of the LPA's decision is also important and is also prescribed by regulations (article 31 of the DMPO).

Where planning permission is granted the notice shall: (a) include a summary of the LPA's reasons for the grant of permission; (b) include a summary of the policies and proposals in the development plan which are relevant to the decision to grant permission; and (c) where the permission is granted subject to conditions, state clearly and precisely the LPA's full reasons for each condition imposed, specifying all policies and proposals in the development plan which are relevant to the decision. The imposition of conditions on a grant of a planning permission is addressed in Chapter 5.

Where planning permission is refused, the notice shall state clearly and precisely the LPA's full reasons for the refusal, specifying all policies and proposals in the development plan which are relevant to the decision.

The notice is important because if consent is granted then the notice defines the extent of that consent and will refer to the plans to which it relates. This may become important if the LPA later alleges through enforcement action, for example, that what has been developed is not the same as what was granted consent for. Conversely, if consent is refused then the reasons for refusal as specified in the decision notice form the basis for deciding whether to appeal the refusal. On appeal, the applicant/appellant is attacking (and the LPA is defending) those reasons, so it is important they are clear and precise to ensure both sides know what they are arguing about.

The substance of how planning applications are determined, i.e. what the LPA must and may consider is considered in Chapter 4. However, there are two more types of applications that need to be addressed in this chapter on process – applications for retrospective consent and applications for conservation and listed building consent.

3.11.1 Retrospective consent

Section 73A of the TCPA 1990 allows for consent to be granted on application to the LPA for development carried out before the date of the application. The development may not have planning permission at all, it may have permission but for a limited period (which has expired) or it might not comply with a condition imposed when consent was granted.

The purpose of section 73A of the TCPA 1990 is to allow for the regularisation of the planning situation in circumstances where the LPA has decided that enforcement action is not expedient.

Section 73A of the TCPA 1990 allows for consent to be granted either from the date on which the development was carried out or from the end of the (expired) limited period for which consent was originally granted. In effect, this section allows for application for a retrospective grant of consent.

The procedure for applying for a retrospective consent is similar to an application for prospective consent, although there are some differences.

The requirements of article 6 of the DMPO – provision with the application of plans and drawings – does not apply to applications made under section 73A(2)(c) of the TCPA 1990 – development that does not comply with a condition – but, otherwise, article 6 does apply. As does the requirement to provide a design and access statement, specified in article 8 of the DMPO.

In respect of conditions, it should be noted there is a separate specific power under section 73 of the TCPA 1990 which allows for applications to be made and for consent to be granted for development without compliance with conditions. This is a more flexible and useful section for an applicant who wishes, in effect, to change or remove a condition because it can be made prospectively. Section 73A, however, only applies to the situation where the non-compliance with the condition has already occurred and the developer has, in theory at least, taken the risk of the LPA taking enforcement action against him.

3.12 Conservation area consent

Conservation areas are those parts of an LPA's area which have been designated as such by the LPA on the basis that they are 'areas of special architectural or historic interest the character or appearance of which it is desirable to enhance' (section 69 of the Planning (Listed Buildings and Conservation Areas) Act 1990 (LBA 1990), often referred to as the Listed Buildings Act 1990).

The purpose of conservation area designation is to provide an enhanced level of planning protection to an area, i.e. one which is physically wider than the protection offered to individual buildings by listing. What is protected by conservation area designation can include the spaces between buildings, how buildings are used, groupings of buildings or how paths, boundaries, etc are laid out; what is protected may not be of architectural interest but, instead, be of historic interest.

Within conservation areas, planning control is generally more stringent so as to provide greater protection for what has been designated as being of special architectural or historic interest. This means, for example, that the LPA is placed under a duty (by section 72 of the LBA 1990) to ensure 'special attention shall be paid to the desirability of preserving or enhancing the character or appearance of' the conservation area, when exercising its planning functions. This includes, of course, determining planning applications.

It also means that the demolition of certain buildings in a conservation area requires consent, known as conservation area consent, by reason of section 74 of the LBA 1990. Further, the unauthorised demolition of a building in a conservation area that does not fall within one of the exceptions to conservation area control is a criminal offence.

Procedurally, an application for conservation area consent must be made on a variant of the standard application form. There are other differences too. If the LPA, on receipt of an application (except for an application for retrospective consent), thinks that the development of land would affect the character or appearance of a conservation area then the application must be publicised under the Planning (Listed Buildings and Conservation Areas) Regulations 1990 (SI 1990/1519).

In practice, conservation area consent is quite often sought in conjunction with an application for a 'standard' planning consent in circumstances where, for example, the applicant wishes to demolish a building in a conservation area in order to replace it with a new building.

3.13 Listed building consent

Listed buildings are buildings, objects or structures which because of their special architectural or historic interest are included on a list of such buildings compiled or approved by the Secretary of State. The listing of a building confers on it the greatest level of protection that the planning system can bring. Accordingly, planning control over works to listed buildings is particularly stringent.

Section 7 of the LBA 1990 provides that:

> ... no person shall execute or cause to be executed any works for the demolition of a listed building or for its alteration or extension in any manner which would affect its character as a building of special architectural or historic interest, unless the works are authorised under section 8.

It is a criminal offence to contravene section 7 of the LBA 1990, punishable potentially with a maximum sentence of 2 years imprisonment and/or an unlimited fine. The LBA 1990 criminalises not just demolition, but also alteration or extension of a listed building. As befits their status in the planning system, one can see that the protection afforded to listed buildings is greater than to buildings in a conservation area, which are in turn themselves protected to a greater extent than 'ordinary' buildings, i.e. those neither listed nor within a conservation area.

It is important to note that the requirement for authorisation of works to a listed building – listed building consent – is distinct from and additional to planning control as it applies to all buildings. What this means is that where the proposed works to a listed building are development as defined in section 55 of the TCPA 1990, planning permission *and* listed building consent will be required. In some circumstances, works to a listed building will not be development and so will not require planning permission but will nonetheless require listed building consent. It is important to note also that it is not possible to apply for an outline listed building consent. This is because any application concerning a listed building must provide enough detail for an assessment to be made at the application stage of the impact the works would have on the building.

The procedures for applying for listed building consent are different. A particular form of the standard application form must be used and the publicity, notification and consultation requirements are governed by the Planning (Listed Buildings and Conservation Areas) Regulations 1990 rather than the DMPO.

Design and access statements are required for listed buildings applications. Further detail on the effect of Listed Building and Conservation Area consents is set out in Chapter 5. How LPAs determine the types of applications dealt with in this chapter is explained in Chapter 4.

4 How Planning Applications are Determined

In many ways this is the most important chapter of the book. The LPA has discretion whether to grant permission for any application properly made that comes before it, and the fundamental question which is usually asked of advisers to applicants is whether consent is going to be granted. Therefore, to know or at least to have a good idea how the LPA is likely to exercise that discretion lies at the heart of the advice which an adviser can give.

4.1 Process – who makes the decision?

The power to determine planning applications is given to the LPA by section 70 of the TCPA 1990.

However, in practice, an LPA may receive hundreds or even thousands of applications each month and in consequence LPAs must, and do, have arrangements in place for handling such large numbers of applications.

Arrangements for local authority decision-making generally vary across the country, but in broad terms the most important decisions taken by a local authority across all areas of responsibility, such as for example setting the budget annually, are often reserved to a meeting of the full council, which is attended by all elected members of the authority. However, full council meetings usually only take place once a month or less which is far too infrequently to deal with all of the council's business.

In consequence, therefore, most local authorities have traditionally organised themselves into a number of committees, each with responsibility for particular areas of the authority's work, such as planning, education, social services, licensing, etc. There are then sub-committees of the main committees which may focus on a smaller geographical area or a narrower aspect of the main area of work. The committees and sub-committees are made up of a smaller number of elected members. This principle still generally holds in authorities where the newer forms of local government organisation, with mayors or executive arrangements, for example, are in place.

So, for planning, it may be that the most strategic long-term (and infrequent) decisions are still taken by a meeting of the full council, for example the adoption of a new plan or the grant of planning permission for a particularly large or contentious development that affects the whole of the LPA's area. The rationale is that the most important decisions require the highest level of decision-making.

The bulk of the planning work of the council is likely to be delegated to the planning committee, which would oversee the determination of the majority of applications and much of the plan-making. Commonly, it would arrange the determination of applications by further delegating to planning sub-committees with responsibility for, say, specific wards in the council's area. It is not unusual in a busy LPA for the planning sub-committees, of which there may be two or three, to meet every fortnight.

The purpose and effect of delegation in this way is both to increase the capacity of LPAs to determine applications, by increasing the number and frequency of meetings that are held, and also to increase the democratic input by allowing greater opportunity for applicants or objectors to see decisions being made in public and for them to contribute to those decisions by addressing the meetings.

4.2 Officer report

Typically, elected members serving on a committee or a sub-committee are informed about the decision they must make by an officer's report. This report should set out all of the relevant factual, policy and legal background to the decision in hand before rehearsing arguments for and against whatever is proposed and usually coming to a conclusion in the shape of a recommendation. It is only a recommendation because the elected members are the ones who actually make the decision; they may accept the officer's recommendation or they may reject it.

The officer's report is a very important document and in planning decisions can be very extensive. Typically, an officer's report for a planning decision would be prepared by a professionally qualified town planner in the employ of the council. It would set out in detail a description of what is being proposed, the relevant planning history, the results of public consultation, the relevant national and local planning policies that apply, and then a discussion of the merits of the scheme. In effect, this is the part of the report where a planning judgment is made by the officer. He will assess all aspects of the proposed development against relevant policy and other material considerations and reach an overall judgment about whether or not the scheme should be granted consent, and if so what conditions should be imposed.

All the members of the committee or sub-committee who are to make the decision will be provided with the officer's report in advance and this forms the basis of discussion at the meeting. In many LPAs officers' reports are published on the website in advance of the meeting; they are essentially public documents. Meetings are generally open to the public unless there are confidential matters for discussion, in which case the public may be excluded.

4.3 Conduct of meetings

Each LPA has its own protocol about who may address a meeting but, in general, the applicant and an objector may be allowed to speak – often only for a short period, perhaps as little as 5 minutes each. The purpose of allowing speakers is to give them the opportunity to persuade the decision-makers – the members of the committee – of the merits or otherwise of a scheme.

4.4 Delegated authority

However, there could never be enough meetings of committees and sub-committees held to deal with all the applications an LPA receives, even in a very quiet rural area without much development. This is a function of both the number of applications made and the time and resources, in the shape of preparation of officers' reports, etc that are consumed by holding meetings of committees and sub-committees, as well as the time commitment of the members of the committee that each meeting requires.

In consequence, all LPAs operate a scheme of delegated authority. This means that the authority to determine certain applications is delegated to specific officers and the decision does not come in front of the elected members at all. In the same way that all decisions of committees and sub-committees are taken using powers delegated ultimately from the full council, so delegated authority allows officers to take decisions using powers also delegated from the same source. Whilst the benefits for the efficient administration of the LPA are obvious – speed of decision-making and greatly reduced cost chief amongst them – at once it can also be seen that there is reduced democratic accountability with this method. This is because officers are not elected, they are employed by the LPA and are not therefore responsive to the electorate through having to seek re-election. However, the practicalities of determining the large number of applications for planning permission demand such a scheme of delegated authority is established in each LPA.

The scheme of delegation specifies posts or job titles, rather than named individuals, for example, Head of Development Management, as being authorised to determine applications without reference to a committee.

There are safeguards built in to the system. In order to be lawful, all schemes of delegation – whether from full council to committees or to sub-committees, as well as to individual officers – must be set out in a publicly available document so that the authority of the decision-maker – whether an individual or a committee – is clearly established in advance.

Also, most LPAs have a protocol whereby if there is any level of public concern, as expressed in a certain number of objections being made to an application, for example, then the protocol is likely to require that the decision may not be taken by an officer under delegated authority and the determination must be made by a committee or sub-committee. In this way it can be ensured that a scheme that may be contentious or divisive is determined by a committee of publicly accountable councillors in the full gaze of the interested public.

Just as an officer must prepare a report for the committee if the decision is to be taken by a committee, so must the officer record the considerations in the same way if the decision is to be by delegated authority taken by the officer himself. Usually, this is done by the officer preparing a delegated report which sets out all the considerations taken into account before reaching a decision. Note it is, of course, a *decision* under delegated authority because the officer is actually determining the application, not making a recommendation to members. The purpose of the delegated report is to ensure that the officer exercising delegated authority takes proper account of all that he should, just as if a report were being prepared for consideration by councillors.

There is an additional safeguard, in that internal arrangements usually require the report to be checked and approved by at least one other senior officer before the decision is made. Thus the planning decision may never simply be taken by a single officer alone.

In practice, the great majority of planning decisions taken by an LPA are by delegated authority. Although they are necessarily the smaller scale and less contentious ones, the great volume of decisions taken in this way make the system extremely important. It allows for LPAs to focus their limited resources on the larger and more difficult decisions that come before it.

4.5 Member overturns

A not infrequent, but often very contentious, occurrence is when an officer's report to a committee of elected members makes a recommendation about a particular development proposal which is not followed by the decision-making committee, which is the converse of the officer's recommendation. This is known as a 'member overturn' because the members have overturned their officers' advice. It can happen in either direction, so an officer may recommend refusal of a scheme but members decide to grant it permission or, more commonly, officers recommend that permission is granted for something only for members to refuse to grant consent.

Member overturns are contentious because they illustrate the different roles and sometimes perspectives of the LPA's officers who are almost always professionally qualified town planners, and their elected members who are not. An officer is, as this chapter illustrates, quite heavily constrained in what he can recommend in response to a planning application by the terms of the development plan and other material considerations; his recommendation is, and is intended to be, predictable. One of the main points of having published policies is to give applicants a measure of certainty about the prospects for their application.

Members, on the other hand may well be motivated by other considerations. Since they are not professional planners they may well not be so aware of the constraints referred to. Whilst an officer can focus purely on an objective assessment of the planning merits in the making of his recommendation, an elected member may well be subject to political pressure; for example, what is proposed may be extremely unpopular locally and may be dominating local political discourse that in a way that is very hard for the member to ignore.

That said elected members can, and sometimes do, bring a perspective to a planning judgment that an officer may not understand. It may be, for example, that a member has a better understanding of how a particular streetscape or building is appreciated or how a building for which the use is proposed to be changed is valued by the community in its current use.

There is no requirement for a committee to accept its officers' recommendations. If there were, there could be no democratic accountability in planning, it would be a purely managerial technical exercise undertaken by the 'expert' town planners with little scope for influence by the community. However, notwithstanding that they have rejected their officers' advice, members must decide an overturn on proper planning grounds or the decision would be vulnerable to appeal and, more generally, the predictability of outcome to the applicant would be destroyed.

4.6 Costs against local planning authorities

The way in which the system seeks to ensure that member overturns are not made on spurious, non-planning, grounds is through the effect of the costs regime which polices the appeal procedure. It does this by requiring reasonable behaviour on all those involved in the appeal process, on pain of a costs award to the party found to have behaved unreasonably. It is commonly an issue in the case of a member overturn because an applicant dissatisfied with a decision which results from a member overturn is likely to exercise the statutory right of appeal, thereby bringing the conduct of the council into the realm of the costs regime.

The operation of the costs regime is governed by CLG Circular 03/2009: *Costs Awards in Appeals and Other Planning Proceedings* (TSO, 2009) (CLG Circular 03/2009), which specifically addresses member overturns in these terms:

> Planning authorities are not bound to accept the recommendation of their officers. However, if officers' professional or technical advice is not followed, authorities will need to show reasonable planning grounds for taking a contrary decision and produce relevant evidence on appeal to support the decision in all respects. If they fail to do so, costs may be awarded against the authority.

Also particularly relevant to member overturns, because they do often concern judgments of the sort here described, is this advice from CLG Circular 03/2009:

> Planning appeals often involve matters of judgment concerning the character of appearance of a local area or the living conditions of adjoining occupiers of property. Where the outcome of an appeal turns on an assessment of such issues it is unlikely that costs will be awarded if realistic and specific evidence is provided about the consequences of the proposed development. On the other hand vague, generalised or inaccurate assertions about a proposal's impact, which is unsupported by any objective analysis, are more likely to result in a costs award.

4.7 Powers

Section 70 of the TCPA 1990 sets out the power of the LPA to determine planning applications, in a deceptively simple way:

(1) Where an application is made to a local planning authority for planning permission—

    (a) subject to sections 91 and 92, they may grant planning permission, either unconditionally or subject to such conditions as they think fit; or

    (b) they may refuse planning permission.

(2) In dealing with such an application the authority shall have regard to—

    (a) the provisions of the development plan, so far as material to the application;

    (b) any local finance considerations, so far as material to the application; and

    (c) any other material consideration.

(3) Subsection (1) has effect subject to section 65 and to the following provisions of this Act, to sections 66, 67, 72 and 73 of the Planning (Listed Buildings and Conservation Areas) Act 1990 and to section 15 of the Health Services Act 1976.

While section 70 of the TCPA 1990 sets out the basic powers of the LPA either to grant permission with or without conditions or to refuse permission, the section also imposes a number of other duties on the LPA which may affect the exercise of its powers.

In section 70(1)(a) of the TCPA 1990 reference is made to sections 91 and 92. Section 91 requires any planning permission to be granted subject to the condition that the development to which it relates must be begun not later than 3 years after the date on which permission is granted. Section 92 requires that an outline permission is granted subject to the condition that any reserved matter application is made within 3 years of the date of the grant of outline permission and that the development itself to which the permission relates must be begun within 2 years of the final approval of the reserved matter or, if on different dates, the last such matter to be approved; this is to prevent the planning system from becoming clogged up with elderly consents which have not been implemented.

Additionally, the LPA may impose such conditions as it thinks fit. Conditions are dealt with in more detail in Chapter 5, but it should be noted that the LPA has far from a free hand since all conditions are required to be both legally valid and, as a matter of policy, necessary, relevant to planning, relevant to the development to be permitted, enforceable, precise and reasonable in all other respects. There is extensive and detailed guidance on conditions in CLG Circular 11/95: *Use of conditions in planning permissions* (DCLG, 1995), together with model conditions addressing the most common situations where a condition may be appropriate, which are expected to be used.

Local finance considerations, referred to in section 70(2)(b) of the TCPA 1990, are defined as meaning, in essence, either a grant from central government or a sum the LPA will or could receive in payment of the Community Infrastructure Levy (CIL).

The reference to section 65 of the TCPA 1990 in section 70(3) imposes a duty on the LPA to take into account representations received in response to the publicity and notification. This makes sense; there would be no purpose in requiring the LPA to publicise or advertise an application and then to allow it to ignore the results of that exercise. The detail of the requirements placed upon LPAs to advertise, notify and publicise applications is addressed in article 13 of the DMPO and discussed in Chapter 3, para 3.9.4.

Various further additional duties are imposed by section 70(3) of the TCPA 1990 through reference there to parts of the LBA 1990 which reflect the additional considerations which accompany applications for development in conservation areas or affecting the setting of a listed building. So, in respect of the former, the LPA must pay special attention to the desirability of preserving or enhancing the character or appearance of a conservation area; and in respect of the latter it must have special regard to the desirability of preserving the listed building or its setting. In both cases the LPA must also, as for development not within a conservation area or affecting a listed building, take account of representations arising from publicity given to the applications.

4.7.1 The development plan

The development plan is defined in section 38 of the PCPA 2004. In Greater London it has three elements – the spatial development strategy, which is commonly known as the London Plan produced by the Mayor; the development plan documents taken as a whole which have been adopted or approved in relation to the area, which is commonly known as the LDF; and the neighbourhood development plans which have been made in relation to the area.

Neighbourhood development plans are a new concept introduced by the Localism Act 2011 as part of the localism agenda. The newly created power allows for either a parish council or a neighbourhood forum, equivalent to a parish council in areas where there is no parish, to propose planning policies for the development and use of land in the neighbourhood through publication of a neighbourhood development plan. If supported in a referendum of the local area, the neighbourhood development plan must be brought into force by the LPA. However, it can only be brought into force in that way if it meets conditions, including that it has regard to national planning policy and is in general conformity with the strategic policy in the LDF, usually expressed in the Core Strategy.

Outside London the development plan comprises, in effect, the development plan documents taken as a whole which have been adopted or approved (the LDF) and neighbourhood development plans which have been made. Regional strategies remain as part of the development plan outside London, but government has made it clear that these will be abolished by Order using powers made under the Localism Act 2011, subject to the outcome of environmental assessments underway at the time of writing.

There are a number of other considerations which affect the discretionary power the LPA has when determining planning applications, but the constraint that is most important is imposed by section 38(6) of the PCPA 2004 which, together with section 70(2) of the TCPA 1990, establishes what is often described as the primacy of the development plan.

Section 38(6) of the PCPA 2004 is in these terms:

> If regard is to be had to the development plan for the purpose of any determination to be made under the planning Acts the determination must be made in accordance with the plan unless material considerations indicate otherwise.

Section 70(2) of the TCPA 1990, set out above, specifically requires LPAs to have regard to the development plan; it can be seen that section 38(6) then requires that the determination must be made in accordance with it, unless material considerations indicate otherwise. The effect of these two provisions is to give the development plan an enhanced status in determining planning applications.

What this means is that if an application comes before an LPA for a sort of development, say family housing in a particular part of its area, and there is a policy which encourages just that sort of housing there, then the permission would ordinarily be granted unless there was good reason for not granting consent. So, for example, if the access to the highway for the particular family housing proposal is not satisfactory, that would clearly be a material consideration which may indicate that consent should not be granted in that particular case.

4.7.2 Material considerations

It is clearly important to understand what are 'other material considerations'. In essence, they are relevant planning considerations, something which has a bearing on the planning judgment that must be made when a particular application is being determined. A common interpretation of the phrase is that provided in the case of *Stringer v Minister of Housing and Local Government* [1971] 1 All ER 65:

> In principle, it seems to me, that any consideration which relates to the use and development of land is capable of being a planning consideration. Whether a particular consideration falling within that broad class is material in any given case will depend on the circumstances.

Government guidance, *The Planning System: General Principles* (ODPM, 2005), puts it this way:

> All the fundamental factors involved in land-use planning are included, such as the number, size, layout, siting, design and external appearance of buildings and the proposed means of access, together with landscaping, impact on the neighbourhood and the availability of infrastructure.

Where there are other material considerations then the same Government guidance indicates that the development plan should be the starting point and other material considerations should be taken into account in reaching a decision.

It is important to note that what is or is not a material consideration is ultimately a matter for the determination of the courts. In the great majority of planning decisions, the issue is less whether a planning consideration is material, but rather how much weight should be given to it. This is a matter for the decision-maker. The decision-maker is initially the LPA; it must decide whether to grant permission and, if so, whether to impose conditions. If that decision is appealed, then the decision-maker becomes the Secretary of State, in the great majority of cases, in the shape of a Planning Inspector.

To revert to the example above of the application for family housing which is supported by policy but has problems with access to the highway, it may be that having considered all the circumstances the decision-maker finds that the access problems are not sufficiently serious to require that permission is refused or that the problems can be overcome with a condition. Conversely, he may take the view that in all the circumstances the problem with access to the highway is sufficiently serious that the application must be refused, notwithstanding the policy in favour. This judgment about the seriousness of the access problems is one of weight.

The primacy of the development plan is supported by a number of other mechanisms. For example, if an application is one that does not accord with the development plan, then it must be publicised as such and this makes it a 'paragraph 2 application' for the purposes of publicity. Thus more extensive publicity is required than for other sorts of application. Also, for certain larger applications over a specified size the LPA does not propose to refuse, there is a requirement placed on the LPA to notify the Secretary of State and send him the details of the application. In this way the Secretary of State is given the opportunity to call-in the application for his own determination.

The costs regime at appeal also serves to reinforce the position of the development plan. CLG Circular 03/2009, already referred to, indicates that it may well be an unreasonable exercise of the right to appeal if an LPA's refusal of permission is appealed where the proposal is 'obviously not in accordance with the statutory development plan and no, or very limited, other material considerations are advanced with inadequate supporting evidence to justify determining otherwise'. Conversely the LPA may be liable for costs if it is found that it unreasonably refused permission for an application that should have been granted permission because it was in accordance with the development plan.

Whilst the development plan itself benefits from the statutory prominence afforded it by section 38(6) of the PCPA 2004, the emerging policies of LPAs may also be taken into account in determining planning applications, although they will attract less weight. The reason emerging policies may be considered is partly because of the prominence that the development plan attracts and because of the time taken for a policy to emerge through the various stages of consultation before it is formally adopted by the LPA. It would make no sense for there to be a 'cliff edge' between the pre-eminence of the adopted development plan and for no weight to be attached to any fresh thinking or new policy direction emerging from the LPA. Emerging policy can indicate the direction of the LPA's thinking before the very lengthy process of formal adoption of a plan is complete. Generally, the more advanced towards adoption a policy is, the more weight can be attached to it.

4.8 Government policy – national planning policy framework

Clearly, government policy is and always has been a material consideration. As described in Chapter 1, para 1.8.2, this is one of the main ways in which government exercises control over individual LPAs in their operation of the planning system. This has historically been done primarily through the government publishing PPGs and, more recently,

PPSs, which usually gave very detailed policy guidance on separate planning topics, such as green belts, housing or renewable energy.

In a dramatic departure from this practice, in March 2012 the government published a single relatively short document that replaced the great majority of PPGs and PPSs. The new document is called the NPPF, which seeks to do in 65 pages what was previously done in over a thousand pages. The brevity of the NPPF is its main characteristic and this is deliberate on the part of the government. The idea is that before the publication of the NPPF, national planning policy was scattered across dozens of different documents and hundreds of pages and was, in consequence, inaccessible to the communities it was intended to serve. Planning policy, so the thinking goes, had become the preserve of the specialist professional planner and lawyer. The NPPF is intended to remedy that situation.

The NPPF is certainly relatively very short and accessible, but critics have suggested that it is consequently unable to provide the same level of protection to, for example, the green belt and buildings of historic interest as did the far more detailed former PPGs and PPSs for these topics.

Perhaps the most contentious innovation is the introduction of a presumption in favour of sustainable development. This is described as a 'golden thread running through both plan-making and decision taking'. Paragraph 14 of the NPPF puts it this way:

For plan making this means that:

- local planning authorities should positively seek opportunities to meet the development needs of their area;
- Local Plans should meet objectively assessed needs, with sufficient flexibility to adapt to rapid change unless,
    - any adverse impacts of doing so would significantly and demonstrably outweigh the benefits, when assessed against the policies in this Framework taken as a whole; or
    - specific policies in this Framework indicate development should be restricted.

For decision taking this means:

- approving development proposals that accord with the development plan without delay; and
- where a development plan is absent, silent or relevant policies are out-of-date, granting permission unless:

- any adverse impacts of doing so would significantly and demonstrably outweigh the benefits, when assessed against the policies in this Framework taken as a whole; or
- specific policies in this Framework indicate development should be restricted.

Note that the rather cumbersome phrase 'Local Development Documents' has been replaced with the phrase 'Local Plan', referred to in the NPPF. This change was effected by the Town and Country Planning (Local Planning) (England) Regulations 2012.

4.8.1 Sustainable development

Clearly, a great deal turns on what is considered to be sustainable development and the policies in the NPPF as a whole (paragraph 6) are stated to constitute the government's view of what sustainable development means in practice for the planning system in England. Drawing on the five guiding principles set out in the UK Government Sustainable Development Strategy, *Securing the future* (TSO, 2005) – living within the planet's environmental limits; ensuring a strong, healthy and just society; achieving a sustainable economy; promoting good governance; and using sound science responsibly. This is presented in summary (at paragraph 7) as characterised by three dimensions – economic, social and environmental, which give rise to the need for the planning system to perform the following roles:

> An economic role – contributing to building a strong, responsive and competitive economy, by ensuring that sufficient land of the right type is available in the right places and at the right time to support growth and innovation; and by identifying and coordinating development requirements, including the provision of infrastructure;
>
> A social role – supporting strong, vibrant and healthy communities, by providing the supply of housing required to meet the needs of present and future generations; and by creating a high quality built environment, with accessible local services that reflect the community's needs and support its health, social and cultural well-being; and
>
> An environmental role – contributing to protecting and enhancing our natural, built and historic environment; and, as part of this, helping to improve biodiversity, use natural resources prudently, minimise waste and pollution, and mitigate and adapt to climate change including to a low carbon economy.

Paragraph 15 of the NPPF urges all Local Plans to follow the approach of the presumption in favour of sustainable development.

At the time of the publication of the NPPF (and during the consultation period on an earlier draft) there was much press attention on what this presumption would mean, and many critics felt it would amount to a green light for developers to be able to build without constraint. Meanwhile, developers in the shape of house-builders criticise the NPPF's policy of empowering LPAs themselves to assess the need for, and to plan for, housing in their area – a function that was previously done at the regional level through Regional Strategies. This criticism arises because although there is an acknowledged need for more housing, it is often very contentious and gives rise to local objection. This is particularly so in the prosperous south east of England where the need is greatest, with the consequence that LPAs there are reluctant to provide enough sites for housing through their plan-making.

4.8.2 Implementation

It may take many years before anyone can say with any confidence exactly what the impact of the NPPF is, but its effect will be begin to be felt immediately. This is because of the way the NPPF is designed to be implemented. Annex 1, which deals with implementation, emphasises the requirement for applications for planning permission to be determined in accordance with the development plan unless material considerations indicate otherwise, and that the NPPF policies are material considerations for determining planning applications and plan-making with immediate effect, i.e. from the date of publication of the NPPF in March 2012.

Annex 1 goes on to allow 12 months from the date of the publication of the NPPF for decision-makers to continue to give full weight to relevant polices adopted since 2004 even if there is a limited degree of conflict with the policies in the NPPF. This is, in effect, a concession to those LPAs that got on relatively quickly with preparing their LDF according to the new system introduced by the PCPA 2004. It would be thoroughly demoralising for the LPAs involved if their new LDF was all but rendered useless by the publication of the NPPF.

However, at the expiry of that 12-month period, i.e. by March 2013 for those LPAs that have adopted LDF documents, weight should be given to relevant policies in existing plans according to their degree of consistency with the policies in the NPPF – the closer the policies in the LDF are to the NPPF policies, the greater the weight that may be attached. This means that after a year, the age of an LDF and the consequent likelihood of that age meaning it is inconsistent with the NPPF will begin to count against it.

For those LPAs that have not adopted policies since 2004 and those that have not prepared a plan under the new system relatively quickly, there is no period of grace. The policies in the existing plans in those authorities, which may be in the form of local plans or UDPs for example, will be given weight according to the degree of their consistency with the NPPF. The older a policy is, the less likely it is to be consistent with the NPPF.

Because the NPPF is a material consideration for decision-taking, as the document itself emphasises, the decision-maker applying Annex 1 must give it more weight than a pre-2005 plan or a post-2004 plan after March 2013. The net effect of this is greater reliance on the NPPF for individual planning determinations by LPAs.

As has always been the case, decision-makers may place weight on relevant policies in emerging plans, and this is also addressed in Annex 1 of the NPPF. The weight to be attached to emerging plans is dependent on the stage of preparation of the plan, the extent to which there are unresolved objections and the degree of consistency of the emerging policies with those in the NPPF.

LPAs are urged to take the NPPF policies into account in their development plan as quickly as possible, either through preparing a new plan or a partial review.

The overall effect of Annex 1 of the NPPF is to ensure that the government's planning policies are brought to bear on individual decisions across the country as quickly as possible. This will either be through LPAs preparing or revising their own plan to reflect the NPPF or, if not, the NPPF effectively rendering all old plans redundant.

4.9 Planning obligations and community infrastructure levy

When granting planning permission an LPA may also enter into a planning obligation. Planning obligations are governed by section 106 of the TCPA 1990 and for that reason they are commonly known as 'Section 106 agreements'. Put simply, a planning obligation is an agreement between the LPA and the developer for the parties (usually the developer) to do something or forebear from doing something related to the development that is the subject of the planning permission. The purpose of the planning obligation is to overcome a legitimate objection to the grant of permission; the planning obligation is intended to make acceptable in planning terms a development that, without the obligation, would not be acceptable to the LPA.

A planning obligation may either be an agreement or may take the form of a unilateral obligation, which means that the developer has undertaken to do something without the LPA's agreement. The existence of such an obligation is a material consideration in determining the planning application. So an LPA or an Inspector determining an application, for example, for a scheme which creates a need for a certain amount of affordable housing may take into account a planning obligation addressing provision of that affordable housing in deciding whether to grant permission.

By way of example, a development for 200 houses on the edge of a town may be acceptable to the LPA in all respects except for concerns about the capacity of the existing access road to the site. The construction by the developers of a new road that would overcome the planning objection could typically be the subject of a section 106 agreement.

Alternatively, as suggested in former government guidance (Circular 05/2005: *Planning Obligations* (ODPM, 2005)), it may be that the planning obligation would be used to prescribe the nature of a development, that a certain percentage of a housing scheme be affordable or that some additional open space is provided to compensate for its loss as a result of the development the subject of the planning permission. In other cases, the development may necessitate an increase in public transport provision if, for example, a large housing scheme were to be developed on the edge of an existing town. In each case, the rationale would be that without the affordable housing, open space or additional public transport, the development proposed would not meet with the LPA's approval in accordance with its development plan, but with those things it would.

It should be noted that there is clearly an overlap between circumstances where a planning obligation is appropriate and those where a planning condition may be imposed. Planning conditions are discussed in Chapter 5, para 5.6. Government guidance (Circular 11/95: *The Use of Conditions in Planning Permissions* (DOE, 20 July 1995)) is clear that where either may be used a condition should be preferred. This is because there is a statutory right of appeal against the imposition of a planning condition under section 78 of the TCPA 1990, which for obligations there is not. There is also a specific statutory means of enforcing conditions through section 187A whereas enforcement of obligations can be more complicated.

In practice, a very common use of planning obligations has been to secure a sum of money to be paid to the LPA. This is specifically allowed by section 106(1)(d) of the TCPA 1990 but has proven to be unsatisfactory and has led to a reform of the system with the introduction of the CIL regime.

The reason why planning obligations have been found unsatisfactory is because the obligation itself takes the form of a contractual agreement between the parties and very often takes a great deal of time to be negotiated and drafted. As a negotiated settlement between parties, there is no certainty of outcome either – developers are able to strike very different bargains with different authorities for the same sort of development. This in turn contributes to the protracted nature of the negotiations as the developers seeks, for example, to achieve the same advantageous terms that it has secured with LPA B as it had with LPA A.

There was also concern that 'planning gain', as it is known, in the shape of the financial contribution made by the developer to the LPA is perceived amongst the public as a way in which the developer can 'buy' planning consent.

In essence, what planning obligations seek to do is to capture some of the value created by the grant of planning permission for the community affected by the development that is the subject of the planning permission. This is a long standing concern of the planning system but one which the CIL regime aims to tackle in a more predictable and transparent way.

4.9.1 How the Community Infrastructure Levy works

The LPA is required to publish a charging schedule which sets the sum that is to be sought from the developer in respect of particular forms of development. So for example an LPA may set a rate of £X per square metre of residential development or £Y per square metre for office and retail development. The sum paid by the developer in accordance with the rate set is then to be used to provide infrastructure.

The liability for the CIL is broad, it arises on development of buildings which people normally enter, which is most buildings, but excludes those buildings into which people only go intermittently for the purposes of inspecting or maintaining fixed plant or machinery

The rate set must take account of the particular infrastructure needs of the LPA's area and the extent to which existing funding falls short of being able to meet that need. Also, of crucial importance, the rate must strike the correct balance between helping to fund the new infrastructure required and the potential adverse effect of the levy on the viability of the development that is to be levied. It would make no sense if a rate was set that was so high it rendered all development unviable such that the developer decided not to go ahead. In short, the LPA needs to demonstrate that it understands its own infrastructure needs and the ability of developers to sustain a levy before one can be imposed.

The process of setting the levy is subject to public consultation and examination in public. In this way the involvement of the community on whose behalf the levy is imposed is achieved.

'Infrastructure' is defined, at section 216(2) of the Planning Act 2008, as including:

(a) roads and other transport facilities,

(b) flood defences,

(c) schools and other educational facilities,

(d) medical facilities,

(e) sporting and recreational facilities,

(f) open spaces ...

These are the things for which the levy may be sought. In London, a levy has recently been set by the Mayor of London specifically to fund Crossrail, the central London east-west rail link, with those boroughs more directly affected by the proposals collecting more (£50 per square metre of development) than those less affected (£35 or £20 per square metre).

A notable absence from the definition of infrastructure is affordable housing. This is of note because many planning obligations concern the provision of affordable housing, either for its actual provision on the site the subject of the planning application or elsewhere, or in the shape of a financial contribution paid by the developer to the LPA for it to invest in affordable housing elsewhere. The Community Infrastructure Levy Regulations 2010 (SI 2010/948) (as amended) do not allow for a levy to be applied in order to provide affordable housing. This means that if a contribution is to be paid by a developer for affordable housing, this must continue to be done by means of a planning obligation.

Changes have therefore been made to the way in which planning obligations can be used, so that they do not overlap with the CIL levy. What was formerly only guidance about planning obligations is now a legal requirement for their use. They must be:

(a) necessary to make the development acceptable in planning terms;

(b) directly related to the development; and

(c) fairly and reasonably related in scale and kind to the development.

Further, a planning obligation may not constitute a reason for granting planning permission for the development if it provides for funding of something that either is intended to be, or could be, the subject of the CIL levy.

5 The Grant of Planning Permission

A grant of planning permission describes the operations and the use (or both) which the LPA permits to be carried out on land. There may of course be other uses or operations which are permitted development but are outside the scope of the permission. Express planning permission is not required for permitted development.

5.1 Legal effect of a planning permission

Section 75 of the TCPA 1990 describes the legal effect of a planning permission. The main effect is that any grant of planning permission 'enures for the benefit of the land and of all persons for the time being interested in it'. This means that the permission (in most cases) attaches to the land as a benefit and does not belong personally to the landowner.

Under section 75 of the TCPA 1990 the planning permission may, but does not have to, specify the purposes to which the permitted operational development may be put. If no purpose is specified, then the permission 'shall be construed as including permission to use the building for the purpose for which it is designed'. For example, if permission for the erection of a block of flats does not specify that residential use is permitted, this purpose will be inferred from the way in which this kind of development is normally used.

5.2 Interpretation

Sometimes the wording of a planning permission is unclear or ambiguous. It may be necessary to look at other documents for clarification. The extent to which extraneous documents, such as the planning application itself, can be taken into account to help with interpretation was set out by the High Court in *R v Ashford BC ex parte Shepway District Council* [1999] PLCR 12. The main principles are as follows:

1. If the grant of planning permission is clear, unambiguous and valid on its face, regard may only be had to the permission itself, including any conditions, and express reasons for those conditions.

2. This rule excludes reference to the planning application itself, unless this is incorporated by reference in the permission.

3. In order to incorporate the application into the permission, all that is required is wording that informs the ordinary reader that the application is incorporated. For example 'in accordance with the plans and application'.

4. If the wording is ambiguous, it is permissible to look at the application itself and any other relevant extrinsic documents.

5.3 Effect of a planning permission

5.3.1 Who benefits?

In most cases, planning permission 'runs with the land', i.e. it is a property right which remains in place should the ownership of the land change. However, a personal permission – for the benefit of the applicant only – may in some very limited cases be granted, usually on compassionate grounds. The permission will be subject to a condition that it enures for the benefit of the named person only.

Permission personal to a company will hardly ever be granted because while the legal personality of the company remains constant, it is a relatively simple matter to change directorships and shareholders. Therefore, the benefit of the permission cannot be effectively restricted to named individuals.

5.3.2 Extent of the permission

The planning permission should clearly describe what is permitted. Operational development is often described in summary, with reference made to plans which contain the detail of how the development is to be built. If what is built does not accord with the approved plans, then the entire development is considered to be without permission, for the purposes of planning enforcement action.

For example, if a developer obtains planning permission for a block of flats but fails to build it in accordance with the detail of the approved drawings so that the external appearance is different, then the entire fabric of the building, and not just the external façade, will be without planning permission.

5.3.3 Outline planning permission

As explained in Chapter 3, para 3.3, section 91 of the TCPA 1990 permits a developer to apply for outline planning permission. This is a grant of planning permission in principle, subject to a condition that the details (referred to as 'reserved matters') are submitted for later approval by the LPA. The obvious advantage is that the developer is spared the expense of producing detailed plans before finding out whether the LPA will grant permission in principle.

Once outline planning permission is granted, an application for approval of reserved matters is made (including the appearance of the development, means of access, landscaping, layout and scale). The application is made in accordance with article 3 of the DMPO. Under the DMPO the LPA may decline to determine the application for outline permission if it considers that it cannot do so until further details are submitted.

Outline permissions are subject to time limits. Section 92(a) of the TCPA 1990 imposes a 3-year time limit on applications for reserved matters approval, starting with the grant of outline permission. Once reserved matters are approved, the development must be begun within 2 years. However, these time limits can be substituted by shorter or longer periods, as the LPA considers appropriate. Separate conditions on the outline permission may be subject to different time limits.

An outline permission remains valid irrespective of whether not reserved matters are approved. It is possible, as long as the outline permission has not expired, to submit a further application for reserved matters approval or appeal against refusal to the Secretary of State.

5.4 Duration of a planning permission

Section 91 of the TCPA 1990 provides that planning permission shall be granted, or deemed to be granted, subject to the condition that the development to which it relates must be started within 3 years.

This period may be shortened or extended by the LPA, subject to the development plan and any other material considerations. If any challenge is made to the validity of a grant of planning permission (for example third party judicial review in the High Court), the period is extended by one year by virtue of section 91(3B) of the TCPA 1990.

Temporary planning permission may be granted for operational development or material changes of use. In effect the permission will be subject to a condition that the building is removed, or the use ceases, after a specified period of time.

5.4.1 When does development begin?

In order to implement a planning permission and stop time running under section 91 of the TCPA 1990, the developer must carry out a 'material operation', defined in section 56(4), namely:

(a) any work of construction in the course of the erection of a building;

(aa) any work of demolition of a building;

(b) the digging of a trench which is to contain the foundations, or part of the foundations, of a building;

(c) the laying of any underground main or pipe to the foundations, or part of the foundations, of a building or to any such trench as is mentioned in paragraph (b);

(d) any operation in the course of laying out or constructing a road or part of a road;

(e) any change in the use of any land which constitutes material development.

Pursuant to section 56(2) of the TCPA 1990, time stops running on the earliest date that a material operation comprised in the development commences.

If no such material operation is started within the specified time limit, then the development is treated as not authorised by the permission. Relatively minor operations are sufficient, for example in *Malvern Hills District Council v Secretary of State for the Environment* [1982] JPL 439, the Court of Appeal held that pegging out the line and width of a road was a material operation within section 56(4)(d) of the TCPA 1990 and, therefore, marked the beginning of the development. Subsequent removal of the pegs does not cancel out the operation, for example in *Aerlink Leisure Ltd (in liquidation) v First Secretary of State* [2004] EWHC 3198 (Admin), the High Court held that the Inspector had misdirected himself in finding that the removal of pegs used for the laying out of an access road meant that the operation was insufficiently permanent to fall within section 56(4)(d).

Very minor (*de minimis*) operations will not be material for the purposes of section 56 of the TCPA 1990. The question is one of fact and degree in each case, but the proportional relationship between the cost and scale of the operation in question and the development as a whole is not the deciding factor. In *Thayer v Secretary of State for the Environment* [1992] JPL 264, the Court of Appeal held the Inspector was wrong to conclude that creating a 12-foot gap in a hedge and carrying out some minor ground works in preparation for the erection of a house and garage was not a material operation.

Whether the intention of the developer is to commence development or merely stop time running under section 91 of the TCPA 1990 is irrelevant.

5.4.2 Completion notices

Section 94 of the TCPA 1990 applies where development is begun within the time limit specified in the relevant condition, but not completed within that period. The permission does not remain in place indefinitely – if the LPA considers that the development will not be completed within a reasonable period, a 'completion notice' may be served. The effect of the notice is that the planning permission expires at the end of the period stated within it. This period cannot be less than 12 months after the notice takes effect. The notice must be served on the owner, occupier and any other persons likely to be affected. The LPA may withdraw the notice at any time.

5.5 Changes to an existing planning permission

Certain changes can be made to a planning permission after it has been granted, subject to the following rules.

5.5.1 Non-material changes

On application by a person with a legal interest in the land to which the permission relates (i.e. an owner or tenant) the LPA may make non-material changes to the wording of the permission pursuant to section 96A of the TCPA 1990. In deciding whether the change is material, the LPA must consider the effect of the change, together with the effect of any previous changes made, on the planning permission as originally granted.

The changes which can be made include imposing new conditions or altering or removing existing conditions.

5.5.2 Revocation of a planning permission

Under section 97 of the TCPA 1990, the LPA may revoke the grant of a planning permission before the development is complete if it is considered expedient to do so having regard to the development plan and any other material considerations. The work already carried out is not affected.

Permission for a change of use may also be revoked before the change has taken place. The LPA is liable to pay compensation for any wasted expenditure arising from the revocation, and any loss or damage directly attributable to it.

Orders under section 97 of the TCPA 1990 must be confirmed by the Secretary of State unless all parties likely to be affected have notified the LPA in writing that they do not object to the Order, in which case an expedited procedure takes place under the provisions of section 99. The validity of the Order may be challenged in the High Court within 6 weeks of its confirmation pursuant to section 288(3). It may not otherwise be questioned in any other proceedings whatsoever, so it is not amenable to judicial review. The power to revoke is rarely used.

5.6 Planning conditions

By virtue of section 72 of the TCPA 1990, conditions may be imposed on a grant of planning permission. Conditions may be imposed for two purposes:

1. For regulating the development or use of any land under the control of the applicant (whether or not it is land in respect of which the application was made) or requiring the carrying out of works on any such land, so far as appears to the LPA to be expedient for the purposes of, or in connection with, the development authorised by the permission.

2. For requiring the removal of any building or works authorised by the permission, or the discontinuance of any use of land so authorised, at the end of a specified period, and the carrying out of any works required for the reinstatement of land at the end of that period.

The wording of the statute grants LPAs a wide power, but it is important to note the three main restrictive principles which apply to conditions. They must:

- fulfil a planning purpose;
- fairly and reasonably relate to the development;
- not be manifestly unreasonable.

See the decision of the House of Lords in *Newbury DC v Secretary of State for the Environment* [1980] 2 WLR 379.

The LPA is required to 'state clearly and precisely their full reasons for any planning condition imposed' under article 31(1)(iii) of the Town and Country Planning (General Development Procedure) Order 1995

(SI 1995/419). However, failure to do so does not of itself render the condition invalid.

5.6.1 Planning purpose of conditions

Conditions must further a planning purpose, not some ulterior (albeit connected) goal. For example, a condition that the occupants of a residential development must be drawn from the council's housing waiting list was found to be *ultra vires* because, in effect, it placed the council's housing responsibilities on the developer and was an interference with its private ownership (see *R v Hillingdon LBC ex parte Royco Homes Ltd* [1974] 2 WLR 805).

Similarly, while the requirement for a development to provide open space can be imposed by condition, there can be no further requirement for the open space to be dedicated to the public as, again, this would limit the rights of the legal owner.

Valid conditions fulfil a wide range of planning purposes. For example, a limitation on the hours during which deliveries may be made to business or industrial premises is common. This would be for the purpose of protecting neighbouring occupiers from disturbance in the early morning and late at night. The protection of residential amenity is a well recognised planning purpose.

5.6.2 Relationship to the development

Conditions cannot impose requirements which do not fairly and reasonably relate to the development for which permission is granted. However, as the wording of section 72(1) of the TCPA 1990 makes clear, conditions may be used to regulate *any* land in control of the applicant, regardless of whether it is within the application site. This means that conditions relating to neighbouring land, in control of the applicant, may still fairly and reasonably relate to the development.

For example, it would be reasonable to require additional parking facilities to be provided on land outside the application site if the need arises from the development permitted, but not if the need already exists. However, where permission is granted for intensification of a use which is likely to generate a material planning impact, such as additional noise disturbance, then it could be appropriate to impose a condition to mitigate the effect of the noise.

A condition need not apply to the whole of the development for which permission is granted.

Conditions may also regulate off-site activity, as long as it is within the applicant's control. In *Davenport v London Borough of Hammersmith and Fulham* [1999] 2 PLR 96, a condition preventing cars under the applicant's control from being parked on a section of street outside the development was held to be lawful.

Conditions modifying the development

Conditions which modify the proposed development can be imposed as long as the result is not a fundamentally different development. The leading case of *Bernard Wheatcroft Ltd v Secretary of State for the Environment* [1982] JPL 37 sets out the test of lawfulness. If the conditional permission would allow a development which is so changed from what was applied for that individuals who were consulted about the original application should have the right to comment on it, then it is unlawful. In that case, a condition was imposed reducing a housing development from 420 to 250 houses on a smaller site – all interested parties had had the chance to express their opposition in principle, the reduction in size made no material difference and the conditional permission was lawful.

Conditions can also limit existing use rights without the payment of compensation, as confirmed by a line of authority beginning with *Kingston-upon-Thames Royal London Borough Council v Secretary of State for the Environment* [1973] 1 WLR 1549. In that case it was held that:

> A condition imposed in exercise of the express power to regulate the use of, or to require the carrying out of works on, land other than the land in respect of which the planning application was made, must, in the nature of the case, encroach upon the applicant's established rights over that other land, which, but for that condition, he would continue to enjoy free of any such regulation or requirement (see the judgment of Bridge J at paragraph 1557 A–B).

5.6.3 'Grampian' conditions

A condition which prevents development from starting before an event which is not wholly within the developer's control has occurred is called a 'Grampian' condition, after the decision of the House of Lords in *Grampian Regional Council v City of Aberdeen* [1984] JPL 590. The condition in question required a road closure to take place before the development could go ahead.

Such a condition is lawful even if there is no reasonable prospect of it being fulfilled. In *British Railways Board v Secretary of State for the Environment* [1994] JPL 32, a condition that residential development could not go ahead until access over neighbouring land owned by the council was granted, was concluded to be lawful by the House of Lords, even though the council had no intention of granting access.

5.6.4 Personal conditions

It is open to the LPA to impose a condition restricting use or development to a particular individual or group for a specified length of time. In *R (Doncaster Metropolitan Borough Council v First Secretary of State)* [2003] EWHC 995 (Admin), a condition specifying that a caravan site could only be used by Gypsy families for a period of up to 3 years was held to be valid.

5.6.5 Reasonableness

If a condition possesses any of the following characteristics it is likely to be invalid:

- it seeks a financial contribution from the developer;
- it interferes with private property rights (see para 5.3.1);
- it is so uncertain as to be unintelligible;
- it is unenforceable.

Financial contributions

A condition which requires the payment of money or some other kind of consideration from the developer is unlawful. This is to be distinguished from financial and other contributions which are made by developers by way of a unilateral undertaking under section 106 of the TCPA 1990, or under the Community Infrastructure Levy Regulations 2010 (SI 2010/948) (as amended). These are considered in Chapter 4, para 4.9.

Private property rights

Conditions cannot restrict private property rights, for example, developers cannot be required to construct roads which are used for the benefit of other land. A requirement to construct an ancillary road and permit neighbouring occupiers to use it was found to be unlawful in *Hall and Co Ltd v Shoreham-by-Sea UDC* [1964] 1 WLR 240.

However, conditions can restrict permitted development operations or use. In *City of London Corporation v Secretary of State for the Environment* (1972) 23 P & CR 169, planning permission was granted for change of use from a warehouse to an office, but on condition that the office was used only as an employment agency. Other uses within the same use class (which would be permitted development not requiring permission) were not allowed.

Uncertainty

The wording of a condition must be clear enough for any reasonable person to understand what must be done to comply. Vague language should be avoided, although a condition will not be found invalid unless it is wholly unintelligible. Words will be given their ordinary and natural meaning and should be construed in a 'benevolent manner' (see *Carter Commercial Developments Limited v Secretary of State for the Environment* [2002] EWHC 1200 (Admin)).

In *Barnes v Secretary of State for Communities and Local Government* [2010] EWHC 1742 (Admin), planning permission for a wind farm was granted with conditions intended to mitigate noise. One of the conditions was that in the event of complaints the local authority had to monitor noise levels. The appellant argued that the condition did not specify the monitoring methodology (only that it was to be agreed with the council) and was therefore uncertain. The High Court accepted that reference to specific methodology would have been 'desirable' but, seen in the context of the other conditions, and the principle that conditions should be given effect if it is at all possible to do so, the condition was found to be valid.

However, there is no scope for implying requirements into a condition if they are not apparent on its face. In *Sevenoaks DC v First Secretary of State* [2004] EWHC 771 (Admin), the council granted planning permission for the construction of a golf course, on condition that the developer would supply details of the layout to the council before beginning work. The developer did submit details which were subsequently approved, but the development eventually carried out did not conform to them. The council then issued an enforcement notice alleging breach of the condition. The notice was quashed, and the Inspector's decision upheld in the High Court, on the basis that the condition did not actually require the work to be done in accordance with the details, it simply required the developer to submit them to the council for approval, which he had done. As a matter of common sense, one might assume that the purpose of the condition was to ensure that the work was carried out in accordance with the submitted details, but as the condition did not say so explicitly this requirement could not be implied. Per Sullivan J at paragraph 28:

> Since a planning permission is a public document and breach of a condition may ultimately have criminal consequences if a breach of condition notice and/or an enforcement notice is served/issued and not complied with, it is essential that any obligation by way of a condition is clearly and expressly imposed

Enforceability

A condition which cannot be enforced by the LPA is likely to be unreasonable. In *R v Rochdale MB ex parte Tew* [2000] Env LR 1, planning permission was granted for a business park, conditional upon the developer carrying out work on neighbouring land which it did not own.

Although there is nothing to prevent conditions from being imposed on land outside the application site or outside the developer's control, the conditions must be capable of reasonable enforcement. In this case if the condition was not complied with, the LPA would have had to take enforcement action against third parties (the neighbouring landowners) who gained no benefit from, and may well have objected to, the development. The sensible alternative in this case would be to impose a Grampian condition preventing the development from starting until the required works have been carried out on neighbouring land. It is then up to the developer to secure agreement for the works if he or she is able to.

5.6.6 Effect of invalid condition

If a condition is found to be invalid, it cannot be removed from the permission unless it deals with some collateral or trivial matter and is therefore 'severable'. If it 'goes to the heart of the permission', then the permission itself is rendered a nullity. In *Mouchell Superannuation Fund Trustees v Oxfordshire County Council* [1992] 1 PLR 97, a condition was imposed that the site could only be accessed by a particular road which did not belong to the developer and needed improvements. The condition was found to be unenforceable as the applicant had no control over the road. It went to the heart of the permission because, without the road, the development and associated use could not go ahead. Therefore the whole permission was a nullity.

However, where a condition is found to be unreasonable and therefore invalid, but unconditional permission would not be refused by any reasonable planning authority, the condition can be severed and the permission itself will stand. In *Allnatt London Properties v Middlesex County Council* (1964) 15 P & CR 288, planning permission was granted for an extension to a factory. However, the condition that the extension was only to be used in conjunction with the main building and only by a person or firm currently occupying a light industrial building in the same county, were found to be unreasonable. The High Court concluded that the permission itself was nevertheless valid.

5.6.7 Challenge to planning conditions

If the LPA imposes a condition on a grant of planning permission and the applicant considers it to be unreasonable or invalid for any other reason, an application can be made under section 73 of the TCPA 1990 for permission to develop the land without complying with the conditions originally imposed or complying with different conditions. Appeal against refusal or a section 73 application lies to the Secretary of State. Section 73 cannot be made in respect of time limit conditions where development has not begun within the specified period.

Alternatively, an appeal can be made to the Secretary of State under section 78 of the TCPA 1990. The Inspector will be able to consider whether the condition is justified for planning reasons and whether it is valid in law.

5.6.8 Conditions following appeal

If conditions are imposed by an Inspector on appeal against refusal of planning permission or pursuant to an enforcement notice appeal under section 174(2)(a) of the TCPA 1990, clear reasons should be given.

The Inspector is not required to formulate conditions which are not suggested by the parties. If a condition is suggested which may be valid and resolve a planning difficulty, the Inspector is not bound to consider it explicitly, although in some cases the decision may be reviewable if this is not done.

It is, therefore, important for applicants and authorities to consider what conditions may overcome any objections to the development. If all objections can be overcome in this way, a refusal of planning permission will not be justified and the LPA is at risk of an award of costs against it if permission is granted following a hearing or inquiry.

5.7 Planning permission and other legal interests

Conflict between a planning permission and other public or private interests is not a rare occurrence. For example, planning permission may generate a kind of use which causes a nuisance not envisaged at the time planning permission was granted.

The key principle is that a grant of planning permission does not authorise interference with other private or public rights and does not remove legal liability in these circumstances. In *Barr v Biffa Waste Services Ltd* [2012] EWCA Civ 312, the Court of Appeal confirmed that, short of express or implied statutory authority to commit a nuisance, there was no basis for using a statutory scheme (such as a grant of planning permission) to undermine private law rights.

5.7.1 Private nuisance

Nuisance in law is an unreasonable interference with the use and enjoyment of property. There are two key principles to consider when a use or development authorised by a planning permission is alleged to be causing a nuisance to neighbouring occupiers:

1. In general, planning permission does not authorise nuisance even though it is an inevitable consequence of implementing the permission.

2. However, a grant of planning permission for a major development can change the character of an area for the purpose of determining whether or not something is an actionable nuisance.

In *Hunter v Canary Wharf Ltd* [1997] 2 WLR 684, the House of Lords was asked to determine, *inter alia*, whether interference with television signals was an actionable private nuisance, and whether planning permission for the construction of the Canary Wharf tower authorised it. Overturning the Court of Appeal's finding, the House of Lords held that this was not an actionable nuisance but confirmed that, had it been, planning permission would not have authorised the nuisance. Per Pill LJ at paragraph 669 in the Court of Appeal:

> I reject the submission that the powers and duties conferred on planning authorities [...] are such that in granting planning permissions under their delegated powers they are conferring an immunity in nuisance upon works pursuant to the permissions.

As the existence of a nuisance is always determined by reference to the character of the area, the question of whether a planning permission has changed this character is key. In *Gillingham Borough Council v Medway (Chatham) Dock Co Ltd* [1992] JPL 458, planning permission was granted to redevelop Chatham Dockyard as a commercial port. The only access road ran through a residential area. When the port opened, the increase in the number of commercial vehicles caused substantial disturbance to neighbouring occupiers. This was held not to be a nuisance as the planning permission had fundamentally changed the character of the area. Such a change could also be created by the designation of land for industrial purposes in the development plan.

In contrast, odour arising from the construction and use of two pig houses on a farm was found to be a nuisance because the character of the area had not changed (see *Wheeler v JJ Saunders Ltd* [1995] 2 All ER 697).

5.7.2 Interference with other easements

An easement is a private right that belongs to a piece of land, for example a private access way over neighbouring property to a house. A grant of planning permission cannot authorise interference with this kind of private right. While planning permission is concerned with public and not private interests, the rights of neighbouring landowners are a material consideration which should be taken into account when planning permission is granted. If such considerations are not taken into account, the only recourse against the grant of planning permission itself is a claim for judicial review. However, those affected may also begin injunction proceedings in the civil courts to restrain interference with their private rights. The existence of a planning permission will not be a defence to such a claim.

5.8 Highways

Part X of the TCPA 1990 sets out the LPA and Secretary of State's powers with regard to stopping up and diverting highways to facilitate development.

5.8.1 Orders made by the Secretary of State

Where the LPA acquires and holds land for 'planning purposes' (e.g. compulsory purchase for development to promote the economic wellbeing of the area under section 226 of the TCPA 1990) the Secretary of State may make an order to stop up any public right of way over that land under section 251. The order can be made if he is satisfied that an alternative right of way has been or will be provided, or that one is unnecessary. The order must be publicised and if objections are received then a local inquiry will be held.

5.8.2 Orders made by the local planning authority

Under section 257 of the TCPA 1990 the LPA (or a government department) may stop up or divert a footpath or bridleway if it is necessary in order to enable development to be carried out in accordance with planning permission. Such an order may provide for the creation of an alternative route.

Section 258 of the TCPA 1990 permits the LPA to divert or stop up any public right of way over land it has acquired and holds for planning purposes (the equivalent of the Secretary of State's power in section 251).

The matters to be taken into account in the exercise of these powers are whether the highway is unnecessary or is needed for public use, whether an alternative highway should be provided and whether any public right of way should be reserved. Particular considerations apply to access land (see section 59(1) of the Countryside and Rights of Way Act 2000).

5.9 Listed building consent

A listed building is a building, object or structure which has been judged to be of national importance for its architectural or historic character. The statutory list is compiled under the provisions of the LBA 1990.

Listed buildings are classified into three categories – Grade I, Grade II* (pronounced 'grade two star') and Grade II. Paragraph 7 of the guidance *Principles of Selection for Listed Buildings* (Department of Culture, Media and Sport, 2010) supersedes CLG Circular 1/07: *Revisions to Principles of Selection for Listed Buildings* (DCLG, 2007), but contains the same explanation of the grading system – Grade I buildings are of exceptional interest, Grade II* buildings are particularly important buildings of more than special interest and Grade II buildings are of special interest, 'warranting every effort to preserve them'.

Section 1 of the Planning (Listed Buildings and Conservation Areas) Act 1990 places a duty on the Secretary of State to compile a list of buildings of 'special architectural and historic interest'. These categories are explained as follows in *Principles of Selection for Listed Buildings* (DCMS, 2010):

- *Architectural interest*: to be of special architectural interest a building must be of importance in its architectural design, decoration or craftsmanship; special interest may also apply to nationally important examples of particular building types and techniques (e.g. buildings displaying technological innovation or virtuosity) and significant plan forms.

- *Historic interest*: to be of special historic interest a building must illustrate important aspects of the nation's social, economic, cultural, or military history and/or have close historical associations with nationally important people. There should normally be some quality of interest in the physical fabric of the building itself to justify the statutory protection afforded by listing.

5.9.1 Extent of a listed building

When a part of a building is listed, the whole of the building is subject to the provisions of the LBA 1990. This extends to structures and objects within the curtilage of the building, even if they are not themselves listed, by virtue of section 1(5), which provides that:

> (a) any object or structure fixed to the building;
>
> (b) any object or structure within the curtilage of the building which, although not fixed to the building, forms part of the land and has done so since before 1 July 1948,
>
> is to be treated as part of the building. This is known as 'curtilage listing'.

The effect of this provision, in its earlier form, was considered by the House of Lords in *Debenhams Plc v Westminster City Council* [1986] 3 WLR 1063 in the context of two buildings linked by a tunnel and a bridge, but not otherwise connected to each other. One was listed and one was not. Section 54(9) of the Town and Country Planning Act 1971 (TCPA 1971) provided that:

> for the purposes of the provisions of this Act relating to listed buildings and building preservation notices, any object or structure fixed to a building, or forming part of the land and comprised within the curtilage of a building, shall be treated as part of the building

The House of Lords held that a 'structure fixed to a building' referred to structures ancillary to the listed building (e.g. a garage) and not some other complete building as in the facts of this case. Therefore, the second building belonging to Debenhams was not a listed building by virtue of section 54 of the TCPA 1971.

5.9.2 Definition of the curtilage

The main case on the extent of the curtilage, in the context of a listed building, is *Skerritts of Nottingham Ltd v Secretary of State for the Environment, Transport and the Regions* [1999] JPL 932. The listed building in question was operated as an hotel. A stable block stood in the grounds approximately 200 metres from the main building. The owner replaced the original windows in the stable block with white plastic double glazing. The LPA took enforcement action on the basis that the stable block was included in the listing by virtue of section 1(5)(b) of the LBA 1990. The argument on behalf of the owner was that the curtilage was by definition a small area around a building. The Court of Appeal disagreed, holding that the extent of the curtilage was a matter of fact and degree in each case, and in the case of a substantial building was likely to extend to what would have been ancillary buildings in the past.

However, present use is equally important. In *Sumption v Greenwich London Borough Council* [2007] EWHC 2776 (Admin), the High Court found that a fence built around a newly extended garden to a listed building could not be permitted development. The garden land was attached to the house and 'clearly capable of being used by the owner' even though there was no historical connection.

In *R (Egerton) v Taunton Deane Borough Council* [2008] EWHC 2752 (Admin), the High Court considered whether a barn extension separated from the main listed house by a wall was within its curtilage. Sullivan J referred to the three main factors listed in *Attorney General ex rel Sutcliffe v Calderdale Borough Council* [1982] 46 PCR 399, namely:

(1) the physical 'layout' of the listed building and the structure,

(2) their ownership, past and present,

(3) their use or function, past and present.

and the dictum of Stephenson LJ at page 47 of that case:

> Where they are in common ownership and one is used in connection with the other, there is little difficulty in putting a structure near a building or even some distance from it into its curtilage. So when the terrace was built, and the mill was worked by those who occupied the cottages, and the mill-owner owned the cottages, it would have been hard, if not impossible, to decide that the cottages were outside the curtilage of the mill.

Looking at aerial photograph evidence from the date of listing, Sullivan J concluded that there was a clear physical distinction between the listed farmhouse and the outbuildings, of which the barn was one. It also appeared, on the evidence, that the barn was being used for farming purposes and not as ancillary to the house. Taken together, these outweighed the fact that the buildings were in common ownership at the date of listing, with the result that the barn was not within the curtilage of the farmhouse.

5.9.3 Requirement for listed building consent

While planning control does not extend to the interior of a building, the listed buildings regime does. Great care must be taken to ensure that the requisite permission is obtained before any work takes place. It should also be noted that listed building consent is required for works which would not qualify as development for the purposes of the TCPA 1990 because, for example, they do not materially affect the external appearance of the building.

Under section 9 of the LBA 1990, it is a criminal offence to execute any works for demolition or alteration of a listed building in a manner which would 'affect its character as a building of special architectural or historic interest', without first obtaining consent.

Following the House of Lords' decision in *Shimizu UK v Westminster City Council* [1997] JPL 523, removal of part of a listed building (in that case, internal fireplaces) is to be treated as an 'alteration' and not a 'demolition'.

A prosecution under section 9 of the LBA 1990 will not succeed unless the authority can prove, to the criminal standard, that the unauthorised works affect the special architectural or historic character of the building. This element of the offence is occasionally overlooked – the prosecution must include evidence that character has been adversely affected.

However, the effect on character must be assessed as it exists at the conclusion of the unauthorised works, i.e. the finished product. In *East Riding of Yorkshire Council v Hobson* [2008] EWHC 1003 (Admin), the developer had obtained consent to make alterations to a stable block annexed to a listed building. In carrying out the works, substantial removal of original fabric took place. for which consent had not been given. The block was subsequently reconstructed. The Administrative Court held that the District Judge was correct in assessing the effect on character at the point the work was complete, rather than looking at the dismantling stage in isolation. The District Judge had found that the whole scheme of works did not have a detrimental effect on the character of the listed building and, therefore, the defendant was correctly acquitted.

Keene LJ observed:

> if what is being done by way of works of alteration to a listed building involves both a stage of removal and dismantling and a stage of replacement or rebuilding, it cannot, in my judgment, be right to cease the assessment of the effect of these works of alteration in an artificial manner part of the way through.

However, if it is found that, after completion of the works, the building's special architectural or historic character is affected, then a conviction will result.

Effect on character

There is no fixed type or category of works which are sufficient to affect the character of a listed building. Alterations to the structure of the building, whether internal or external, are likely to affect character. Relatively minor non-structural works may still affect character. In *Newport County Borough Council* [2003] JPL 267, the use of a brightly coloured synthetic paint on the exterior was found to represent an alteration which affected the traditional character of a Grade II listed cottage.

The question of whether minor works qualify as alteration will depend on the extent to which they affect the building's character. For example, repainting an already painted listed building with the same type and colour of paint will not be an alteration. However, painting a previously unpainted building or repainting in a different colour will almost certainly affect character and require consent. The same principle applies to repainting the interior.

5.9.4 Exempted listed buildings

Not all listed buildings are subject to listed building control under the prosecution provisions of the LBA 1990.

Churches

Many churches are listed buildings, however, in many cases the carrying out of unauthorized works cannot give rise to prosecution. Section 60 of the LBA 1990 provides that, *inter alia*, sections 7 to 9 of the Act do not apply to 'any ecclesiastical building which is for the time being used for ecclesiastical purposes'. Section 60(3) provides that a building being used by a minister of religion as a residence from which to perform the duties of office (e.g. a Vicarage) is not to be treated as an ecclesiastical building.

Restrictions on the application of section 69 of the LBA 1990 are found in the Ecclesiastical Exemption (Listed Buildings and Conservation Areas) (England) Order 2010 (SI 2010/1176). Articles 5, 6, 7 and 8 contain the list of ecclesiastical buildings to which the exemption still applies.

Scheduled ancient monuments

Buildings included in the list of ancient monuments are, by virtue of section 61 of the LBA 1990, subject to the controls of the Ancient Monuments and Archaeological Areas Act 1979 only. These include the issue of enforcement notices and stop notices, and prosecution for failure to comply.

5.9.5 Obtaining consent

The procedure for obtaining listed building consent is not very different to obtaining planning permission. A standard application form is used which is available on the LPA's website or the Planning Portal website (www.planningportal.gov.uk). The person making the application does not have to have any interest in the land, but notice must be given to every person who owns the freehold, a long lease or a tenancy with at least 7 years left to run (see the Planning (Listed Buildings and Conservation Areas) Regulations 1990).

The LPA must consult English Heritage on a range of listed building consent and planning applications. These include works in respect of any Grade I or Grade II* listed building, and works for the demolition of a Grade II unstarred building.

The LPA may refuse or grant consent, subject to conditions.

Government guidance

Unlike in the determination of applications for planning permission, the council is not required to take the provisions of the development plan into account when determining applications for listed building and conservation area consent. In planning decisions, LPAs are *required* to take the provisions of the development plan and all material considerations into account, by virtue of section 38(6) of the PCPA 2004. There is no such statutory requirement in respect of the listed building control regime. The only statutory requirement is set out in section 16(2) of the LBA 1990, namely that:

> (2) In considering whether to grant listed building consent for any works the local planning authority or the Secretary of State shall have special regard to the desirability of preserving the building or its setting or any features of special architectural or historic interest which it possesses.

The statutory emphasis is thereby on preservation. Applicable guidance contains the detail on how preservation, and enhancement, should be achieved.

PPS5: *Planning for the Historic Environment* (TSO, 2010) (PPS5) contained the government's policies on conservation of the historic environment. Paragraph 4 explained that the polices set out in the guidance apply to the consideration of the historic environment in relation to the 'other heritage-related consent regimes', i.e. listed building and conservation area control, as distinct from planning control.

Policy HE7 of PPS5 contained guidance on the factors which should be taken into account, which are as follows:

(i) evidence provided with the application

(ii) any designation records

(iii) the historic environment record and similar sources of information

(iv) the heritage assets themselves

(v) the outcome of the usual consultations with interested parties; and

(vi) where appropriate and when the need to understand the significance of the heritage asset demands it, expert advice (from in-house experts, experts available through agreement with other authorities, or consultants, and complemented as appropriate by advice from heritage amenity societies).

The list was by no means exhaustive and the remainder of policy HE7 contained detailed guidance on how these factors should be considered.

The PPS5 policies were intended to substantiate the government's vision and objectives for the preservation of the historic environment, which are set out *The Government's Statement on the Historic Environment for England 2010* (Department for Culture, Media and Sport, 2010). The vision is summarised as being:

> That the value of the historic environment is recognised by all who have the power to shape it; that Government gives it proper recognition and that it is managed intelligently and in a way that fully realises its contribution to the economic, social and cultural life of the nation.

PPS5 has now been superseded by the NPPF. Part 12 'Conserving and enhancing the historic environment', in paragraph 128 requires applicants to:

> describe the significance of any heritage assets affected, including any contribution made by their setting. The level of detail should be proportionate to the assets' importance and no more than is sufficient to understand the potential impact of the proposal on their significance. As a minimum the relevant historic environment record should have been consulted and the heritage assets assessed using appropriate expertise where necessary.

The NPPF echoes the statutory emphasis on preservation – paragraph 136 confirms that this must be given great weight, in proportion to the importance of the heritage asset.

5.10 Conservation areas

The first conservation areas were designated in 1967, in recognition of the fact that areas beyond an individual building or structure had special architectural and historic character, and were deserving of protection. The majority of conservation areas are designated by the LPA. The LPA is required to support the designation by adopting development plan policies applying specifically to the conservation area.

A conservation area is defined in section 69(1) of the LBA 1990 as 'an area of special architectural or historic interest, the character or appearance of which it is desirable to preserve or enhance'.

The words 'preserve or enhance' are repeated in development plan policies applying to conservation areas. For example, development plan policy frequently states that development will not be permitted where it fails to preserve or enhance the character of the conservation area. Some conservation areas, and parts within conservation areas, are of a weaker character and perhaps less intrinsic value than others. This is acknowledged in the NPPF which came into force on 27 March 2012. Paragraph 127 of Part 12 states:

> When considering the designation of conservation areas, local planning authorities should ensure that an area justifies such status because of its special architectural or historic interest, and that the concept of conservation is not devalued through the designation of areas that lack special interest.

Overall, however, Part 12 of the NPPF places a clear positive duty on the LPA to consider the potential negative impact of development in conservation areas. Development which leads to 'substantial harm' to a heritage asset should usually be refused (paragraph 133). However, in the event of 'less than substantial harm' to the heritage asset, this should be weighed against the 'public benefits' of the proposal (paragraph 134).

Both the applicant and the LPA are required to carry out an assessment of the impact the proposed development is likely to have on identified heritage assets.

5.10.1 When is conservation area consent required?

The relationship between the requirement for planning permission and for conservation area consent is not straightforward. By virtue of section 74(1) of the LBA 1990, conservation area consent is required for the demolition of any *unlisted* building in a conservation area. If the building is listed, then listed building consent is required for any works of demolition or alteration but conservation area consent is not needed.

Following the judgment of the House of Lords in *Shimizu (UK) Ltd v Westminster City Council* [1997] JPL 523, conservation area consent is only required if the works to an unlisted building amount to demolition of the entire building. Demolition of a building within a conservation area without consent is a crime.

External alterations (falling short of demolition) to an unlisted building in a conservation area require planning consent unless they are 'permitted development'. In the case of permitted development, planning consent is only required if a direction under article 4 of the GPDO is in place, or it is required by condition on a previous planning permission.

Directions under Article 4 of the Town and Country Planning (General Permitted Development) Order 1995

Under the GPDO, the local authority is empowered to issue a direction (known as an 'article 4 direction') removing permitted development rights. The types of permitted development rights that can be removed in conservation areas are listed in article 5, and include alterations to roof slopes, front doors and painting the exterior of buildings.

Notwithstanding the wording of the GPDO which provides that the LPA may issue an article 4 direction if 'satisfied that it is expedient', paragraph 200 of the NPPF introduces a 'necessity test':

> The use of Article 4 directions to remove national permitted development rights should be limited to situations where this is necessary to protect local amenity or the wellbeing of the area (this could include the use of Article 4 directions to require planning permission for the demolition of local facilities). Similarly, planning conditions should not be used to restrict national permitted development rights unless there is clear justification to do so.

Local Heritage Lists

Local Heritage listing provides communities and local authorities with a means of jointly identifying 'heritage assets' which are valued as distinctive features of the local historic environment. The Local Heritage List is not limited to buildings, it may include a variety of features such as bridges, street furniture and village ponds. These 'heritage assets' are not protected by statute (they are not listed buildings) but their inclusion in list the may be a material consideration in planning decisions. In May 2012, English Heritage published its *Good Practice Guide for Local Heritage Listing*. It contains comprehensive guidance on appropriate selection criteria.

Chapter 6 sets out the avenues of appeal against decisions of the LPA to grant or refuse the consents outlined in this chapter.

6 Appeals against Refusal of Planning Permission

This chapter sets out the procedure for appealing against the LPA's decision not to grant planning permission for operational development or change of use (including listed building and conservation area consent) or refusal to grant a Certificate of Lawful Existing or Proposed Use or Development. The procedure is similar for all.

6.1 Refusal of planning permission

The refusal of planning permission takes the form of a letter setting out the development applied for, the decision to refuse, and the reasons for refusal. The reasons will invariably refer to the provisions of the development plan, and supplementary planning guidance where this is relevant.

6.2 Who can appeal?

Only the applicant for planning permission can appeal against refusal. Appeal lies to the Secretary of State. While the coalition government mooted the idea of a third party right of appeal against planning decisions, it does not appear in the Localism Act 2011. There is no statutory right of appeal against a grant of planning permission by interested parties such as community groups, although such decisions may be subject to a claim for judicial review in the High Court.

The main parties to an appeal are the appellant and the LPA, however, third parties often play an important role.

6.3 The role of 'third parties'

Local residents who oppose an appeal development will usually attend the planning inquiry. In major inquiries, residents should wherever possible try to organise themselves into a coherent group or groups, with a chosen representative. It is not unusual for such residents' groups to be represented by a barrister or solicitor (as the appellant and LPA usually will be), particularly at inquiries into large scale development such as wind farms and power stations.

The term 'third parties' refers to three distinct groups:

1. *'Statutory parties'*: where planning permission is applied for by someone other than the sole owner of land, the landowner or any agricultural tenant may make representations to which the LPA must have regard (section 71(2) of the TCPA 1990). These persons are entitled to full participation in the planning inquiry, including the right to call evidence and cross-examine witnesses.

2. *'Other persons entitled to appear'*: other planning authorities for the area are also entitled to appear at an inquiry, even if they were not the LPA for the decision to refuse planning permission. This category also includes other bodies such as National Parks Authorities, Enterprise Zone Authorities and the Environment Agency

3. *'Any other persons'/'Rule 6 parties'*: any other person is entitled to attend the public inquiry, and any person may speak at the inquiry subject to the Inspector's discretion. Local residents and community groups fall into this category.

'Rule 6 parties' are groups of people such as residents' associations who have applied to the PINS to take a very active part in the inquiry under rule 6 of the Town and Country Planning Appeals (Determination by Inspectors) (Inquiries Procedure) (England) Rules 2000 (SI 2000/1625) (Inquiries Procedure Rules 2000). They will be required to submit a statement of case and may submit proofs of evidence.

The PINS guidance for rule 6 parties dated November 2011 explains the rule 6 process. It acknowledges that:

> Rule 6 parties can offer significant value to the inquiry process. However this is only the case where Rule 6 parties add substantively to the case being made by the local planning authority and/or the appellant/applicant. It is not beneficial to the inquiry for Rule 6 parties to repeat evidence given by other parties.

Rule 6 status is not normally granted to individuals.

6.4 Who determines planning appeals?

The majority of planning appeals in England and Wales under section 78 of the TCPA 1990 are determined by a Planning Inspector appointed by the Secretary of State for Communities and Local Government. Jurisdiction for the determination of the appeal is transferred from the Secretary of State to an appointed Inspector.

6.4.1 Recovered jurisdiction

In some major development appeals jurisdiction is 'recovered' by the Secretary of State – this is known as a 'recovered appeal'. Appeals may be recovered at any stage before the Inspector has issued a decision. The criteria for recovery are set out in the Written Ministerial Statement for 20 June 2008 on Planning Appeals. The Secretary of State will 'consider' recovering a range of appeals including; those which involve proposals for development of major importance having more than local significance and proposals giving rise to substantial regional or national controversy including those which are of major significance for the delivery of the government's climate change programme and energy policies. The list in the Ministerial Statement is not exhaustive. The Secretary of State has discretion whether to recover appeals.

In practice, a recovered appeal is heard by a Planning Inspector at a public inquiry, although the appeal may proceed by way of written representations or a hearing. The usual procedural rules apply to the inquiry process (see paras 6.5.2 onwards). Following inquiry the Inspector issues his recommendation to the Secretary of State, who then makes and issues a final decision on the appeal.

6.5 Deciding to appeal against refusal of planning permission

The first step is to assess whether the council's reasons for refusing the application are sound, and likely to be upheld on appeal. This involves analysing whether the LPA has properly and fairly applied all the relevant development plan policies.

Where feasible, it is better to negotiate alterations to the proposed development which will overcome the council's reasons for refusal, and submit a further planning application, rather than pursue an appeal. This option is may particularly suit householders who do not have the resources to instruct professional advisers to manage an appeal on their behalf. A second fee may not have to be paid to the LPA in these circumstances (see Chapter 3, para 3.9.2).

Planning appeals are subject to a costs regime which may result in an order for the appellant to pay the council's costs, or vice versa, arising from any unreasonable conduct. Deciding whether the prospects of success are sufficient to warrant an appeal is not an easy process without previous experience of planning law and practice. In all but the simplest appeals, it is advisable to take advice from a planning consultant or specialist lawyer at this stage. The advantage of engaging a planning consultant is that he or she will be able to advise on the prospects of an appeal succeeding, as well as providing credible evidence to the Inspector on the planning merits of the development.

Planning Aid provides some free advice for those who cannot afford professional fees (www.rtpi.org.uk).

6.5.1 Does the proposal accord with the development plan?

This question lies at the heart of any planning appeal. It derives from section 38 of the PCPA 2004, which provides that all planning decisions 'must be made in accordance with the development plan, unless material considerations indicate otherwise'. The answer is a matter of planning judgment – if the matter is decided on appeal, the Inspector will apply his judgment and reach a decision. There is often not an obvious answer to the question. Appeals on large scale applications involve weeks, months and sometimes years of conflicting expert evidence on the planning merits.

Even if a development does not accord with the letter of a particular development plan policy, this does not mean that permission will not be granted. The Inspector will weigh all the relevant factors in the balance. Where the planning benefits (such as regeneration or the provision of additional housing) are clear, a minor infringement of development plan policy will not justify a refusal. Equally, where there is unlikely to be any materially negative planning impact, a technical breach will not justify a refusal.

The Inspector will also take the appellant's proposed planning obligations, if any, into account where they meet the test set out in regulation 122(2)(a) of the Community Infrastructure Levy Regulations 2010 (SI 2010/948) (as amended), i.e. if they are:

(a) necessary to make the development acceptable in planning terms;

(b) directly related to the development; and

(c) fairly and reasonably related in scale and kind to the development.

See Chapter 4, para 4.9.1 for further detail on the CIL.

6.5.2 When and how to appeal

When should the local planning authority issue its decision?

Appeals against refusal of planning permission, or conditions on a grant of planning permission, are made under section 78 of the TCPA 1990.

An appeal may also be made on the basis of non determination, i.e. where the LPA fails to issue a decision on a planning application within eight weeks (or longer if an extension of time has been agreed). The 8-week period is prescribed by the DMPO and runs from the date that application fees are paid.

In the case of applications for consent for conditioned matters on an earlier grant of planning permission, the authority should give its decision within 8 weeks of the application being received.

'Major development' applications as defined in article 2(1) of the GPDO must be determined within 13 weeks of being made. Time runs from the date of validation by the LPA.

A longer period of 16 weeks applies in the case of applications requiring environmental assessment (see regulation 32(2) of the Town and Country Planning (Environmental Impact Assessment) (England and Wales) Regulations 1999).

If these time limits have expired without the LPA making a decision, the right to appeal under section 78 of the TCPA 1990 arises in the same way as if the application had been determined and refused.

Time limits for appeals

Notice of an appeal must be lodged within 6 months of the decision to refuse planning permission. An appeal can only be brought by the applicant, so there is no third party right of appeal against refusal or, indeed, against a grant of permission.

However, where enforcement action is also being taken in respect of the same, or substantially the same, development for which planning permission was refused, the time limit for bringing an appeal under section 78 of the TCPA 1990 is shortened to 28 days.

The appeal must be made on a standard form which is available from the Planning Portal website (www.planningportal.gov.uk). The appeals page contains useful guidance on how the form should be completed. In addition to being completed online, a hard copy must also be sent to the LPA.

Householder Appeals Service

A different procedure applies to householder appeals. The Householder Appeals Service (HAS) is an expedited appeal procedure for appeals in respect of straightforward residential development and change of use.

The decision is made on the basis of written representations from the appellant and the council. The procedure is set out in the Town and Country Planning (Appeals) (Written Representations Procedure) (England) Regulations 2009 (SI 2009/452). This is a comparatively low-cost, high-speed procedure. The HAS is suitable for:

- appeals relating to an application for development such as dwelling house extensions, alterations, garages, swimming pools, walls, fences, vehicular access, porches and satellite dishes (this list is not exhaustive);
- appeals against the refusal of householder applications for planning permission, as well as refusal of any consent/agreement/approval required by or under a planning permission, development order or local development order;
- appeals against an LPA's decision to refuse to remove or vary a condition or conditions attached to a previous planning permission for householder development.

It is not suitable for all types of appeals by householders, for example it is not appropriate in the case of non-determination and appeals against conditions imposed on a grant of planning permission.

Householder appeals must be submitted within 12 weeks of the decision being appealed, using the Householder Planning Appeal Form also available on the Planning Portal website. The shortened 28-day period applies if the council has also taken enforcement action against the same, or substantially the same, development.

6.5.3 What to include in an appeal form

The Planning Portal website guidance sheet *How to complete your planning appeal form* explains what information should be included in the appeal. A site ownership certificate, showing who owns the land, must be provided when the appeal form is submitted. The most detailed section will be the grounds of appeal. This should set out, as concisely as possible, why the appellant considers that the provisions of the development plan are complied with, are not relevant or are overridden by material planning considerations. The grounds should be under 3,000 words. The guidance lists the essential supporting information which must be provided at this stage.

Further relevant supporting information, such as letters from neighbouring occupiers who support the proposal, should also be submitted.

6.5.4 Choice of procedure

There are three possible methods of determining a planning appeal – written representations, hearing or public inquiry. The appellant's preference should be indicated on the appeal form; the council's observations are also taken into account but the procedure is ultimately decided by the PINS.

The criteria for deciding the correct procedure are set out in Annex C to the Procedural Guidance – Planning Appeals and Called-in Applications (PINS 01/2009). Appellants are expected to have regard to the criteria when choosing the appeal procedure.

Written representations

This procedure is suitable where:

- the grounds of appeal and issues raised can be clearly understood from the appeal documents plus a site inspection; and/or
- the Inspector should not need to test the evidence by questioning or to clarify any other matters; and/or
- an EIA is either not required or the EIA is not in dispute.

The potential costs involved are considerably lower than for hearings or inquiries. Written representations will be suitable where the planning issues are fairly straightforward and there is no real conflict of evidence.

Hearing

If the criteria for the written representations procedure are not met, for example because there is some evidential matter which is not agreed, the hearing procedure will be suitable if:

- there is no need for evidence to be tested by formal cross-examination; and
- the issues are straightforward (and do not require legal or other submissions to be made); and
- the appellant should be able to present his or her own case (although the appellant can be represented if he or she wishes);
- the appellant's case and that of the LPA and interested persons is unlikely to take more than one day to be heard.

Inquiry

If the criteria for the hearing procedure are not met, then a local inquiry will need to be held. The inquiry is a formal hearing where parties are usually (but not invariably) represented by advocates. Factual evidence is given on oath and witnesses are subject to cross-examination. Evidence and submissions are heard in formal order. Where a proposed development has generated a significant amount of local opposition, the council will usually indicate that a local inquiry should be held. This gives local residents and other third parties the opportunity to give evidence.

6.5.5 Alterations to the proposed scheme

Following submission of the appeal, the appellant may propose changes to the scheme and invite the Inspector to grant permission for the new scheme as an alternative to the one that was refused. In deciding whether to accept such amendments, the Inspector will apply the principles set out in *Bernard Wheatcroft Ltd v Secretary of State for the Environment* [1982] JPL 37. *Planning Inspectorate Good Practice Advice Note 09: Accepting amendments to schemes at appeal* (PINS, February 2011) summarises these principles. The central test is whether the development is 'so changed that to grant it would be to deprive those who should have been consulted on the changed development the opportunity of being consulted'. The restriction on amendments made at the appeal stage exists to protect the interests of third parties.

6.6 Inquiries procedure

The procedure for most planning inquiries is set out in the Inquiries Procedure Rules 2000. Major infrastructure projects such as airports and power stations are subject to a special procedure set out in the Town and Country Planning (Major Infrastructure Projects Inquiries Procedure) (England) Rules 2005 (SI 2005/2115).

The Inspector has power under section 79(6A) of the TCPA 1990 to dismiss an appeal on the grounds of the appellant's undue delay in complying with any of the procedural requirements. However, the appellant will be warned of this consequence and given time to comply with any specified steps.

6.6.1 Preliminary stage

As soon as practicable after the decision is made to hold an inquiry, the Secretary of State will send a notice in the form of a letter to the LPA and the appellant to that effect. An inquiry date will also be set. The date of this letter is known as the starting date. In complex appeals a pre-inquiry meeting may also be held to discuss timetabling and deal with any preliminary matters.

6.6.2 Statement of case

Within 6 weeks of the starting date the LPA and the appellant must submit a statement of case to the PINS and any statutory parties. This is also known as the 'rule 6 statement'. It is intended to be a comprehensive summary of each party's case. Care must be taken to set the case out clearly as significant matters raised later on, without good reason, may trigger an application for costs.

6.6.3 Statement of common ground

The LPA and the appellant are required by rule 14 of the Inquiries Procedure Rules 2000 to prepare a statement of common ground. This document summarises the points on which the parties agree (often limited to a description of the development, the planning history of the site, and the relevant policies), lists the factual matters which are not agreed, and summarises the issues which remain to be determined at the inquiry. It is not unusual for appellants to treat the statement of common ground as a further opportunity to put their case; this is unhelpful and will simply delay agreement from the council. The statement of common ground should be drafted as neutrally as possible.

6.6.4 Proof of evidence

Rule 13 of the Inquiries Procedure Rules 2000 provides that 'any person entitled to appear at an inquiry, who proposes to give, or to call another person to give, evidence at the inquiry by reading a proof of evidence' shall provide a proof of evidence no later than 4 weeks before the inquiry date.

Rule 11 of the Inquiries Procedure Rules 2000 lists the persons entitled to appear at an inquiry. They include the appellant, the LPA, representatives of any statutory party and the Parish Council if it made representations to the LPA regarding the application. However, this is not prescriptive – the Inspector is entitled to allow any other person permission to appear (i.e. speak) at the Inquiry, and this permission is not to be unreasonably withheld.

Rule 11 of the Inquiries Procedure Rules 2000 also provides that persons entitled to appear may represent themselves or be represented by 'any other person'. There is no limitation on rights of audience at planning appeals.

Evidence is usually given by the appellant or his or her planning consultant and any other professional witnesses (e.g. architect). The officer who considered the application will usually give evidence on behalf of the LPA. Neighbouring occupiers and other interested parties will also be allowed to speak.

On a strict reading, rule 13 of the Inquiries Procedure Rules 2000 only requires proof of evidence to be prepared if the person proposes to give evidence by reading it. In practice, however, proof of evidence will almost invariably be provided by all the witnesses for the main parties. Failure to do so is likely to result in adjournment and an application for costs. Without pre-exchanged proof of evidence, it is more likely that one or more of the parties will be unable properly to address what the undisclosed evidence states and will need an adjournment to consider the new evidence.

A short summary should be provided if a proof of evidence is longer than 1500 words.

All the documents on which the person giving evidence proposes to rely should be attached to the proof and submitted with it. There is some very limited scope for submitting documents after the proof of evidence, as late as the inquiry day itself. However, this is a high-risk strategy as it is entirely within the Inspector's discretion whether to accept late evidence. There is little consistency of approach between Inspectors, and much depends on whether the other parties object.

If late evidence is sent to the PINS for the Inspector's attention after the deadline but before the Inquiry, it will invariably be sent back. Documents are emailed to the case officer, not the Inspector. This usually results in the party wishing to submit the evidence having to apply to the Inspector at the inquiry. Late evidence which necessitates an adjournment will almost inevitably lead to an application for, and more often than not an award of, costs against the party providing the evidence late.

6.6.5 The inquiry

The running order for planning appeal inquiries under section 78 of the TCPA 1990 is normally as follows, although it may be altered at the Inspector's discretion:

1. *Inquiry opened by the Inspector*: the Inspector introduces himself and states his qualifications, e.g. chartered Town Planner. He then asks who speaks on behalf of the council and the appellant. If the parties are represented by advocates, they introduce themselves and then

state the names of the witnesses they will be calling to give evidence.

The Inspector then summarises the main issues. At this stage he may ask the parties' advocates for submissions on preliminary points that are unclear from the written material submitted.

There may be further housekeeping matters to deal with such as ensuring that sufficient copies of documents are available. The Inspector asks for letters of notification of the inquiry and ascertains that the parties have all received any representations sent to the PINS in response.

The LPA should provide an attendance sheet which everyone present at the inquiry should sign. A new sheet is needed for each day of the Inquiry.

The Inspector also asks for the signed statement of common ground.

The parties' advocates are usually asked for their estimates on how long their evidence in chief and cross examination will take, so that the Inspector can properly manage the progress of the inquiry.

2. *Opening statements*: the advocates may each make an opening statement. In short and straightforward inquiries this is often omitted. For more complex inquiries the advocates normally provide a written opening statement.

3. *LPA's evidence*: each party is obliged to present its case as succinctly as possible and avoid wasting inquiry time, starting with the LPA officer who gives evidence first. The council's advocate introduces the officer to the inquiry by reading out his name, qualifications and experience from the introduction to the proof of evidence. The advocate then asks the officer to read out his summary proof. The Inspector does not usually object to relevant parts of the main proof also being read out or further questions being put to bring out the main points in the council's case. There is no advantage to be gained from reading out long tracts of agreed material, for example applicable policy, and the Inspector normally stops this, although it is common if there are many members of the public present at the inquiry who may not have seen the proofs of evidence in advance. This first part of a witness' evidence is known as 'examination in chief'. The officer is then cross-examined by the appellant, or his or her advocate if there is one, for the purpose of challenging the evidence or opinions with which the cross examining party disagrees and putting his or her own case.

Third parties will also have the opportunity to cross examine the council's witness if appropriate.

4. The calling advocate is then allowed to re-examine the witness and the Inspector also asks questions if there are any points he wishes to clarify:

5. *Appellant's evidence*: the process is reversed; the appellant and any witnesses give their evidence in chief, and are subsequently cross-examined by the council's advocate and third parties. The Inspector asks questions if necessary.

6. *Third parties*: the Inspector then asks the third parties to speak. If unrepresented, third parties do not usually provide proof of evidence but rather read out statements or letters they have already submitted to the PINS and the LPA. They may be cross examined by the main parties' advocates, and asked questions by the Inspector.

7. *Conditions session*: once the evidence is complete, the Inspector moves on to look at conditions which may be imposed if permission is granted. This is not an indication that the Inspector has decided to grant permission – he usually states this explicitly. The parties' advocates do not usually take an active role during the conditions session, and the discussion is led by the witnesses for each side. The Inspector also takes an active part.

8. *Closing submissions*: the LPA makes its closing submissions first; the appellant has the last word. Closing submissions are an opportunity to summarise the important points and deal with matters which arise from the evidence. The length of closing submissions depends on the complexity and the length of the inquiry. Inspectors expect written closing submissions in inquiries in most cases, and certainly for those which last longer than one day.

9. *Costs applications*: after closing submissions the Inspector asks 'if there are any other applications to be made'. This is the cue for the advocates to indicate whether they intend to make applications for costs. It is good practice, encouraged in CLG Circular 03/2009, to warn the other side of a costs application as far in advance as possible, and ideally to present it in writing.

10. *Site visit*: the Inspector normally visits the site accompanied by representatives from both parties, even if he has made an unaccompanied visit first. This is an opportunity to point out relevant features of the site and surroundings – the Inspector does not hear any more evidence or submissions from the parties. Third parties usually attend the site visit. Inspectors are often very willing

to view a site from a neighbouring property to assess the impact of the appeal scheme, if asked to do so.

11. *Decision*: the Inspectorate sends out the Inspector's written decision after the close of the inquiry. A decision is normally issued within the region of 6 to 8 weeks. Any costs decisions are sent out at the same time but in a separate letter.

6.7 Costs

The Inspector's power to award costs is contained in section 250 of the Local Government Act 1972, which applies to the TCPA 1990. Costs awards may be made regardless of the outcome of the appeal procedure. Thus a successfully appellant may, nonetheless, be ordered to pay the costs of the LPA if he or she has conducted his or her case unreasonably and vice versa. Formerly, costs were not awarded in appeals decided by written representations but this is no longer the case.

The criteria for determination of costs applications are set out in CLG Circular 03/2009. The basic principle is that costs may be awarded if a party has acted 'unreasonably' and the other side has incurred costs as a result. The costs regime is disciplinary but not punitive – unreasonable conduct which does not result in wasted expense is not punishable by an award of costs. There is no equivalent in public inquiries to the presumption in the civil courts that costs 'follow the event'.

Examples of unreasonable conduct by the LPA are:

- pursuing unsubstantiated reasons for refusal;
- ignoring the development plan or established case law;
- relying exclusively on third party opposition to refuse an application for planning permission.

Examples of unreasonable conduct by appellants are:

- failure to pursue an appeal or attend a hearing or inquiry;
- pursuing an appeal where the development is clearly contrary to the development plan and there are no, or very limited, material considerations in favour of granting permission;
- refusing to enter into planning obligations which are clearly necessary to make the development acceptable.

Awards to or against third parties will only be made in exceptional circumstances.

6.8 Inspector's conduct

A planning inquiry is a public hearing at which justice must not only be done, but seen to be done. If the Inspector does not give a party a proper opportunity to present his or her case, or does not listen to what is being said, the resulting decision may be quashed on appeal to the High Court.

The PINS publishes the *Inspector's Code of Conduct*, which contains 11 principles including that 'inspectors should not be fettered with predetermined views and should not judge cases before they have considered the evidence'. Complaints about the Inspector's conduct may be made to the PINS Quality Assurance Unit. The unit will investigate complaints impartially but cannot overturn the Inspector's decision. The unit may investigate the complaint during the inquiry (if it is lengthy) or after it has closed. Often, the investigation will delay the issue of a decision.

6.8.1 Inspector's powers on appeal

Section 79 of the TCPA 1990 sets out the Inspector's powers on appeal. They are to:

(a) dismiss the appeal;

(b) vary or reverse any part of the LPA's decision;

(c) grant planning permission for the development without conditions;

(d) grant planning permission for the development with conditions.

In respect of costs applications, the Inspector may dismiss the application, make a partial award of costs or make a full award.

It is important to note that the whole of the LPA's decision is reviewable by the Inspector. Even if the appeal is against the imposition of a condition on a grant of planning permission, the Inspector may of his own initiative refuse permission for the entire development. If the Inspector intends to proceed in this way, the parties should be given adequate notice so that the appellant has the opportunity to withdraw the appeal. Appellants may alternatively apply for the condition to be discharged under section 73 of the TCPA 1990, if necessary by appeal to the Secretary of State, so the risk of losing the entire permission does not arise.

Giving reasons

The Inspector is under a duty to give clear reasons for his decision. The reasons need not be detailed but they must be 'adequate and intelligible' (see *Ellis v Secretary of State for the Environment* (1974) 31 P & CR 130). While the Inspector must have regard to every material consideration, the decision letter need not mention them all. A decision which is not based on evidence is likely to be quashed. In *Banks Horticultural Products v Secretary of State for the Environment* [1980] JPL 33, the Inspector refused an application for planning permission for peat extraction, for the reason that an alternative source of peat existed closer to the appellant's main customer. The Inspector had no information on the availability, suitability and cost of peat on that alternative site, and had therefore made his decision on the basis of unfounded assumptions. The decision was quashed.

6.8.2 Listed building and conservation area appeals

Appeals against refusal to grant listed building or conservation area consent follow a very similar timetable and procedure to appeals under section 78 of the TCPA 1990. Guidance is available on the appeals page of the Planning Portal website. Appeals must be made within 6 months of the LPA's decision. The same choice of procedure applies.

6.8.3 Lawful development certificate appeals

Section 195 of the TCPA 1990 grants the right to appeal against the LPA's decision to refuse (or fail to determine) a lawful development certificate application. The right to appeal applies only if there is no valid enforcement notice then in force. The correct form and guidance notes are available on the Planning Portal website. The onus of proof is explicitly placed on the appellant, who must prove on the balance of probabilities (not the higher criminal test of beyond reasonable doubt) that the development is immune from enforcement action. Appellants in CLEUD or CLOPUD appeals must take care to present a clear and coherent case. If there is no or insufficient evidence supporting the appellant's case, and the LPA has substantial evidence showing that the development is not lawful, the LPA will usually apply for an award of costs

6.9 Appeals to the High Court under section 288 of the Town and Country Planning Act 1990

Any person, not just the main parties to an appeal, who is aggrieved by the outcome of an appeal under section 78 of the TCPA 1990 may make an application for review of the Inspector's or Secretary of State's decision to the High Court under section 288. Appeals can only be made on points of law or procedure – the High Court cannot review an Inspector's decision on the facts of an appeal or their implications unless this part of the decision is manifestly irrational.

Appeals under section 288 of the TCPA 1990 must be made within 6 weeks of the decision. There is no scope for extending time.

A detailed review of the grounds which may found successful appeals on points of law is beyond the scope of this book. In summary, an Inspector's decision will be outside the powers of the TCPA 1990 if it is based on an illegality, is irrational or is procedurally improper. If the High Court finds that the Inspector's decision was outside his powers under the TCPA 1990, it has discretion to quash the decision but is not compelled to. The remedy is discretionary depending on the totality of the circumstances and the overall justice of the case.

A decision may fall under the illegality ground if the Inspector misapplies the law, for example by misinterpreting the provisions of the development plan. Alternatively, the Inspector may have failed to take a relevant material consideration (e.g. amenity impact on neighbouring occupiers) into account. Conversely, if an irrelevant consideration is central to the Inspector's decision it may be also open to review.

The Inspector's decision may be irrational if it is so unreasonable that no reasonable Inspector, properly directing himself, could have come to it. The classic case on unreasonableness in public authority decision-making is *Associated Provincial Picture Houses v Wednesbury Corporation* [1947] 1 KB 223 – 'Wednesbury unreasonable' is shorthand for this definition of unreasonableness. A decision may be procedurally improper if, for example, the Inspector has failed to give one of the parties a fair hearing, for example by unfairly restricting cross examination or submissions. This is a high test and, where matters of planning judgement are concerned, usually difficult to meet.

High Court appeals are complex and potentially very costly, and costs here usually follow the event, i.e. the losing side will be ordered to pay the winning side's costs.

6.9.1 Protective Costs Orders

In some circumstances it is possible to get an Order from the High Court which provides that the appellant will not be responsible for the respondent's costs even if the appeal fails, or that any eventual costs order will be capped to a specified amount.

Directive 83/337/EEC provides in article 10a that in cases to which the Directive applies (including those in which an EIA is a requirement), members of the public with 'sufficient interest' must not be prevented from accessing a judicial review procedure because it is 'prohibitively expensive'. Protective Costs Orders (PCOs) are designed to give effect to this requirement.

PCOs are governed by the 'Corner House' principles, set out in the case of *R (Corner House Research) v the Secretary of State for Trade and Industry* [2005] EWCA Civ 192, [2005] 1 WLR 2600 by Lord Philips MR:

1. A protective costs order may be made at any stage of the proceedings, on such conditions as the court thinks fit, provided that the court is satisfied that:

    i) the issues raised are of general public importance;

    ii) the public interest requires that those issues should be resolved;

    iii) the applicant has no private interest in the outcome of the case;

    iv) having regard to the financial resources of the applicant and the respondent(s) and to the amount of costs that are likely to be involved it is fair and just to make the order;

    v) if the order is not made the applicant will probably discontinue the proceedings and will be acting reasonably in so doing.

2. If those acting for the applicant are doing so pro bono this will be likely to enhance the merits of the application for a PCO.

3. It is for the court, in its discretion, to decide whether it is fair and just to make the order in the light of the considerations set out above.

With regard to the applicant's financial resources, however, the Court of Appeal in *Garner v Elmbridge Borough Council* [2010] EWCA Civ 1006 confirmed that the affordability of proceedings should be assessed objectively rather than against a particular applicant's financial resources. In addition to the principle that the question of whether the proceedings were prohibitively expensive should be assessed against the financial resources of the ordinary member of the public, Sullivan J observed:

> The more intrusive the investigation into the means of those who seek PCOs and the more detail that is required of them, the more likely it is that there will be a chilling effect on the willingness of ordinary members of the public (who need the protection that a PCO would afford) to challenge the lawfulness of environmental decisions

6.9.2 Interim orders

Application may be made under section 288(5) of the TCPA 1990 for an interim order to suspend the operation of the decision until the final determination of the appeal. So for example, the High Court may suspend a planning permission so that development cannot commence until the appeal is dismissed.

Glossary

CIL	Community Infrastructure Levy
Circular 10/97	Circular 10/97: *Enforcing planning control – legislative provisions and procedural requirements*
CLEUD	certificate of lawfulness for existing use or development
CLG Guidance	CLG *Guidance on information requirement and validation*
CLOPUD	certificate of lawfulness for proposed use or development
DAS	Design and Access Statement
DMPO	Town and Country Planning (Development Management Procedure) (England) Order 2010 (SI 2010/ 2184)
EIA	Environmental Impact Assessment
GPDO	Town and Country Planning (General Permitted Development) Order 1995 (SI 1995/418)
HAS	Householder Appeals Service
Inquiries Procedure Rules 2000	Town and Country Planning Appeals (Determination by Inspectors) (Inquiries Procedure) (England) Rules 2000 (SI 2000/1625)
LDF	Local Development Framework
LPA	local planning authority
NPPF	*National Planning Policy Framework*
NSIP	nationally significant infrastructure project
PCO	Protective Costs Order
PCPA 2004	Planning and Compulsory Purchase Act 2004

PINS	Planning Inspectorate
PPG	Planning Policy Guidance note
PPS	Planning Policy Statement
PPS5	PPS5: *Planning for the Historic Environment*
SPZ	simplified planning zone
TCPA 1947	Town and Country Planning Act 1947
TCPA 1990	Town and Country Planning Act 1990
UDP	Unitary Development Plan